Cracking
The Marriage Code

By Jerry Stumpf

THANK YOU PAGE:

Thanks to my sweet wife Elaine for forty years of a wonderful marriage, and our three children Matt, Kristen, & Phillip and their spouses for their dedication to make each of their marriages as good as possible.

Elaine & I thank all those who have attended our "The Best Is Yet To Be!" Marriage Seminars and for their responses to make each new seminar a bit better than the last one.

The encouragement of all my friends at these wonderful sites: 48Days.net

Internet Marriage enrichment pioneers such as Paul & Lori Byerly for their contributions to thousands of marriages through their programs:

www.The Generous Husband.com; and www.The Generous Wife.com; and The Marriage Bed.com.

To Brad and Kate at www.onefleshmarriage.com for their work to strengthen married couples.

Please sign up for our e-newsletter on
www.JerryStumpf.com

TABLE of CONTENTS

JERRY STUMPF

INTRODUCTION

Cracking The Marriage Code: Is it for me?

What if your marriage was the very best it could possibly be? What would that look like?

Not sure how to answer that question? **This book is for you.**

This book is not for you if you are looking for a divorce. If you do not want to work on your marriage, this book is also not for you.

However, do you want a closer, more intimate relationship with your wife? **This book is for you.**

Want to have a more fulfilling sexual relationship? **This book is for you.**

Is respect something that is needed in your marriage? **This book is for you.**

Want more sex? **This book is for you.**

Is there the emotional intimacy that God has in store for married couples? **This book is for you.**

The information contained here has helped many husbands and wives become more interconnected with each other and see each other more clearly.

Above all else, be sure you take action with the insights generated throughout this book!

Cracking The Marriage Code is not simply a book about marriage. It is a practical roadmap to enhance your relationship. It is laid out as a sensible study on how to treat your wife like the princess she dreamed of becoming while she grew up. It is not a clinical study of theories about marriage. Throughout the book, husbands will discover a series of helpful ways to make marriage the best it can become.

My wife, Elaine and I, come from extremely different cultural backgrounds and life experiences. The good news is that, no matter your background, your marriage can become stronger and closer knit together because of your life experiences, giving you a path to follow. *Cracking The Marriage Code: PEP UP YOUR MARRIAGE* contains simple, practical ways in each chapter to enhance any marital relationship. It is designed specifically for husbands who wonder how to better understand and support their wives, and for husbands to enjoy creating deeper memories with their wife.

A critical question to ask about this book for marriage is: *"Why another book about marriage enhancement?"* Simply stated: **"Because people are still having marital problems!"**

If there were already enough materials to solve every couple's issues, we would need no more books, videos, websites, DVDs or CDs on marriage assistance. However, when two people get married, forming a committed relationship, they will eventually have difficulties at some level. This book and the other materials offered through "Cracking The Marriage Code" are aimed at solving issues a man and a woman face in this hyper-busy lifestyle within marriage. We approach helping married couples crack the marriage code and solve their problems from a unique alternative, due to having helped lots of marriages of all age ranges, combined with our own struggles through forty years of marriage. It is designed to help couples benefit from the best life available in their specific situation.

How can a husband and wife make a great marriage out of an existing chaotic situation? For any married couple who is trying to "work it out" in marriage, this book will give you hope. If a husband needs some practical directions for his relationship, this book can help.

Early in our marriage we felt something needed to change. We had to learn from the beginning how to live in different worlds than in the ones we grew up in. Elaine & I come from such dissimilar backgrounds that it is a wonder we became best friends through these years, yet that is precisely what has taken place. In fact, it may be the unique backgrounds that pushed us to develop such a beautiful marriage, since there is a strong commitment to make it work. There is hope for a better relationship no matter what your marriage looks like at this point.

This book is written primarily for men, but I know that couples will read it together and perhaps in some cases only the wife will read it wanting to better understand her husband. It matter not who starts the journey, both men and women can benefit from the stories, from the "PEP PILLS" at the end of each chapter, and from the ideas expressed along the way.

What is so wrong with divorce?

It is a curious circumstance that most people, if not all people, will agree that divorce is bad for all persons concerned. Certainly, as you will later read about me, children suffer from deep embedded scars for many years due to their parents' divorce. Both marriage partners suffer from this separation.

The one most guilty (however a person can asses this fact) knows deep inside that they caused some amount of pain to be poured onto the other. The one who has inflicted the lesser amount of pain, still has pangs of guilt or remorse. The reality? Both spouses are guilty of inflicting pain into all who are associated with this marriage.

One might argue that it is the only solution and yet the experts in this field will mostly agree that there always seems to be a way out if both partners are willing to listen to a trusted trained expert or even a valued couple who have greater insights and life experiences to help the struggling couple.

My point is simplistic: divorce hurts those interconnected with the couple who is looking for a way out. This book is written to assist any couple who is looking for a way to heal, grow and become a model for other fledgling couples to imitate. Study this book as a couple who wants to enjoy the zest and intimate vitality present on your marriage day.

Here is a unique way to study this book together:

A technique for joint study of the hard copy for this book involves two different colored highlighters. He marks the paragraphs or sentences he finds important or has a question about in a blue highlighter. His wife marks her relevant places in pink highlighter. This gives to opportunity for the other person to see what is important to the initial reader. Whenever a section is purple, they both believe that part to be important.

This two-highlighter method gives a basis for discovery and communication, especially for the quieter partner. This more reserved person can open to a highlighted section and say something like, "What are your thoughts about this?" This opens a dialogue in an otherwise omitted territory for the couple.

It also affords each spouse the opportunity to see inside the other partner in a non-threatening fashion, since "Jerry" said this! When using this two-highlighter technique with my wife Elaine early in our marriage, I would open a book to the highlighted part and ask Elaine to read it. I would watch her reaction and then say something like, "Is that right?" or "Do you (think, or feel, or believe) that way?" She would comment, and we had a good discussion based on what a third party said. It was not an assault on either one of us; it opened up some meaningful dialogue. I became much more informed about how my wife stood on a particular subject through this non-threatening process. Give it a try! It could become very positive for your marriage.

Adapt "Cracking The Marriage Code" for YOUR marriage

This book is written for the *typical male and the typical female* in the situations presented. *It is up to each married couple to adapt this information to their personal circumstance.* That is why the "two highlighter" approach is mentioned. Use this book as a matter-of-fact reference guide to develop a deeper level of open communication between each partner, both husband and wife. After forty years of marriage, we still learn new things about each other periodically. So, be patient with each other and learn a bit more at least once a week to enjoy the pleasures God grants when "two become one" in every way a marriage has in store!

Here is a specific challenge as an active participant and not as a passive reader. Read the chapters and begin to do the practical exercises (**PEP PILLS**) at the end of each one. Commit to positive changes for the next 90 days. Evaluate the individual progress as a devoted husband and challenge yourself to become even better during the next chapter. Think about this as a new "workout regimen," where new ideas and techniques are being developed to strengthen new "love" muscles. At the end of each 90 days, evaluate how well the chapters are developing. If at any place along the way, some help is needed, send an email and let me help a bit. It can even be from "anonymous." The greatest "gift" is to see the transformation in your marriage because so much has been invested into the relationship.

Change the lie and create the *"Most Perfect"* marriage possible

For generations, people have been fed the lie that "practice makes perfect." Let's set the record straight on this thought. Only **perfect practice** makes any activity perfect. When a person wants to excel at a certain sport's move perfectly, then they must get a suitable coach who will give the right advice to perfect their incorrect moves and practice properly organized movements. Imagine trying to become the next NBA superstar by finding a kid in a playground who isn't even using the same piece of equipment or type of basketball as the NBA does? It would be much more effective to hire a professional trainer or coach to evaluate the right and the wrong moves being made and give specific advice about incorrect methods for play.

To be the best requires the proper coach and applied discipline over time working on the right moves to be the best possible basketball player. *Cracking The Marriage Code: PEP UP YOUR MARRIAGE* can be the coach that teaches any husband to be the best he can be. Ninety days from now, the application of the principals found within these pages can transform any husband from good to great or great to exceptional!

What relationship is worth more than the covenant called marriage? In the quest to find something worth fighting **for**, just look across the room at your spouse and determine that she is worth committing the necessary time to become the best husband possible. This is a study guide to make marriages the best they can be.

At every situation in life, *"The Best Is Yet To Be!"* So always look for the best from marriage. This is not just a simple formula from Robert Browning, it is solid mantra for couples to follow. Make the marriage relationship better by working on yourself. No matter where the relationship is presently, your marriage can thrive, not just survive. When couples are willing to do whatever it takes to have a wonderful marriage, a great relationship can become a reality. Enjoy this book and be sure to do the "**PEP PILLS**" at the end of each chapter. Let the *FUN* continue!

So let's get started and Crack The *MARRIAGE Code!*

CHAPTER ONE

When "Little House On The Prairie" collides with "Divorce Court"

If you want to learn how to make your life filled with the wonders God has designed for a man and a woman to thoroughly enjoy as a married couple, you have come to the right book. If you are looking for a way out of your marriage, this book is **not** for you. Cracking The Marriage Code is written with the premise that marriage is a lifelong commitment between a man and a woman on a journey to find out all they can about each other as husband and wife.

Why not take pleasure in the journey along the way? Any issues between spouses can be corrected when they are willing to work through the concerns encountered. How long it takes to correct each problem depends upon how deeply entrenched a couple is in these personal issues. This book is written specifically for the male side of the couple, to encourage men to be the best husband they can be.

Some folks waste their life seeking to find "the one," which they believe is out there "somewhere for them," while they have a very special husband or wife who has committed to share their life with them already. Tragically, after a while, that person who they initially believed they were in love with, turns out not to be "the one" they married, or so it seems in their mind.

Here is an alternative, which is not popular among the masses of humanity. When two people get married, whomever they married IS ABSOLUTELY "*THE RIGHT ONE*" for them. Let this premise soak in for a minute.

Marriage was created for two people to dedicate their life to the person they selected to be with for the rest of their life, and their spouse has also dedicated their life to them. Focus on keeping the covenant formed on that special wedding day, and have a wonderful time enriching the relationship bond that was created.

What happens when the honeymoon ends?

A popular question asked by either spouse during a time of frustration in an early stage of marriage is, "Did I marry the right person?" Through this book, you will discover you really did marry the right person. She may appear to come from another planet at times; however, a husband and a wife can learn to enjoy being with each other. Be different than those people who simply endure their life together. Make a difference in the world and determine to learn as much as possible about your wife. Marriage was designed for a man and a woman to completely enjoy each other emotionally and physically developing a relationship which blossoms over time! It does not matter what backgrounds or what distinctive inherent tendencies both partners possess. Each marriage is unlike every other marriage in all the world! Enjoy the beautiful differences that make up that special marriage bond between you and your wife.

Initially, something drew you two together? Was it a physical beauty or something special about your wife's personality? Perhaps it was the way she contorted her face or a certain cute smile she had? What makes a man take a second look at a certain woman and eventually decide to commit the rest of his life to this amazing woman? Whatever it was, after the wedding ceremony, the dust settles and the honeymoon stage is jolted awake by reality. Now, this husband and wife begin to see unmistakably how unlike each other they are in numerous ways. There's a point during which a spouse may question this life-changing decision and pauses to evaluate the stark reality that this lifelong commitment to one single person creates.

This chapter looks at the personal story of my wife and I to prove that no matter the husband and wife's background, any marriage can become a vibrant and peaceful marriage. The personal references will give you a picture of how different two people can be and yet how they can develop into a wholeheartedly joyful life.

There have been many "storms" in our relationship, which were often self-induced. Some of these issues were brought to light many years after the actual events took place. Here are two separate and very different family traditions, which give a hope-filled blueprint to follow for any husband and wife team.

You will find the chapter title **When "Little House On The Prairie" collides with "Divorce Court"** is about our diverse background. Elaine comes from a family where each member was appreciated including mom, dad and all the children. In my family it seemed to be a continuous fight between the four of us. Later on in my life I would become closer to my mom thorough several unforeseen changes in our family. One important idea should become clear as you read through our individual stories. You can develop in a different direction than what your family background suggests.

Elaine's Family Heritage

My wife, Elaine, is from a stable family with 5 brothers and sisters. Her mom and dad were married twenty-four years, before her dad died of cancer when Elaine was in high school in Ludington, Michigan. She grew up in the same house from elementary school through high school. Shortly after her high school graduation, her mom moved to the nearby town. At this stage of life, her mom wanted to downsize her living arrangements, since she was completely alone for the first time in a long time.

As to the stability of her home while Elaine was growing up, her family were regular church-going folk, with her dad being one of the leaders in their congregation. They practiced love for others and love for the immediate family. As adults, most of her brothers and sisters settled in their hometown and still maintain a close interconnected relationship with each other. Her parents were wonderful role models for her family, so Elaine had a blessed upbringing. I did not have the privilege to meet her dad, as he passed away years before I met Elaine. I grew to love her mom a great deal. Her mom was a kind woman and was most happy when her family was in the house, with all children, their spouses, and grandchildren really enjoying each other's company.

I was curious as to how a family this size could be so well adjusted. Through the early years of our marriage, her mom, Grace, would reminisce as to how she and "Dewey" (Elaine's dad) handled their personal issues through several tough financial stages in their life. Grace and Dewey did not argue in front of the kids, even though the children knew at times there was an edge of disagreement in the air. Their family's disagreement style was incredibly different than my family's, as we will point out in the next section.

"As to Elaine's mom and dad, several incidents are close to my heart as they demonstrate Grace's resolve to be committed to her husband's integrity and still keep her children's welfare as a main concern in her heart. In the mid nineteen fifties they lived in Missouri away from their families back in Michigan. Dewey sought work as best he could. It was an anxious time in America's history, since World War II was over and the Korean conflict was escalating. Grace, Dewey, and nine of their children lived as sharecroppers. Four of these children were Elaine's stepbrothers. (Elaine was not yet born at this time.) Dad worked on any job site he found away from the farm while mom and the kids worked the farm. When dad came home, he also worked the farm. After several long, frustrating years, when the oldest boys moved out to find better jobs for themselves, Grace and Dewey could no longer work the farm as needed, so they packed up their meager belongings and went back to

Michigan. The family moved into a corner of the grandparents' barn for a few months. During this time, Elaine was born. Dewey worked through two jobs in nearby factories, and after a few years, they bought the farmhouse about which Elaine has such fond memories.

All through this difficult transition of harsh working conditions, moving back up north, and settling into new housing arrangements, Grace and Dewey kept their disagreements between themselves. As children often do, the children felt each new endeavor was simply a fun adventure. The family heritage is one of financial distress and physical hardships, yet it is chock full of emotional fullness.

While growing up with her five siblings (the step brothers had left to start their own lives), Elaine developed warmhearted memories of the farmhouse with its large garden. She also remembers fondly their short travels across Michigan, all together in their small car, six kids with mom and dad, to see her stepbrother who was suffering from an inoperable brain tumor. In just a few years, Elaine's dad had also passed away.

Years after these tragic incidents, I came into the picture. By this time, Elaine's brothers and sisters were all married and most of them lived near their mom. During the first year of marriage, we also lived in the same town as her family. Each Sunday all the kids and grandkids gathered to eat lunch at "Ma's" house. It was a memorable time, where the entire family enjoyed catching up on the week's activities and reconnecting with each other. Elaine's mom was certainly the bond for this family. I enjoyed seeing firsthand how a family with assorted personalities could come together to enjoy a weekly social environment. These rich occurrences impressed me, as my family history is extremely unlike Elaine's family in size and emotional scope.

My Family Heritage

WOW! My family background is nothing like my wife's upbringing! As you will see, my mom and dad's disagreement styles were not even close to how Elaine's parents worked through family difficulties.

To give a bit of the background, my dad's parents both died when he was very young, at ages nine and eleven respectively. His brother Johnny, raised him. At a very early age, he found regular jobs, since he left school before he finished the eighth grade. At eighteen, he entered the Marines, and at nineteen, he landed on **Guadalcanal Island with the first Marine Division. After World War II, he returned to Glenn Burnie, Maryland. He and my mom had known each other from before the war, and shortly after dad's return to the states, they were married. Dad worked many different jobs, including working for a master carpenter, rehabbing church buildings in Baltimore.** My dad was a very talented carpenter who did not recognize nor appreciate his carpentry expertise.

My mom (Ada) was the oldest of five children and, during her early years, grew up on a farm that she despised. She would scowl whenever a person mentioned "*the good old days*" since she was the one to carry water into the house in a bucket for the family bath, as they had no running water in her farmhouse. Ada was the oldest, that meant she got her bath last. Imagine what that water looked like!

As money was tight, she went to work early in her life to help provide for the family. Therefore, my mom did not finish junior high school. Her mom and dad both worked their farm and other jobs, so much of the responsibility for the family fell to Ada. She grew up on a farm with such a hard life, she vowed never to live that way again when she finally moved into the big city. That "big city" was near Baltimore. When the farm life did not pan out, her whole family moved to a smaller town of Glen Burnie. It was here that she met my dad. As I mentioned, they married shortly after my dad returned from the war. My mom and dad both worked for as long as I can remember. They each had a very strong work ethic.

My dad was of the "old school" where you did your job, and if you worked well, you got paid. Nothing else was expected or rewarded. Do your job and get paid for the job you did. No pat on the back or a "good work!" kind of expression. I am not sure if it was the brutality he witnessed in World War II or what he learned through his upbringing, but he had difficulty in his close relationships. This style carried over to being a father as well: "Just, do your job, son." I do not remember ever hearing positive encouragements like, "You did a good job on the lawn." Mostly it was, "Hey what took you so long?" or, "Here is your next job; get to it!" In this way, dad was very matter of fact when work needed to be done.

Not everything in my childhood was bleak, yet there was just something missing that I could not quite understand for many years. Growing up, I did not appreciate what my parents sacrificed in their lives to provide for my brother and me. Therefore, I did not understand about dad's childhood or his time with the Marines. One stark fact shows this disconnect vividly. I only remember my dad telling me he loved me on two solemn occasions: the first time was at my brother's funeral when I was twenty one and the second time was at the VA hospital about three days before my dad died. Later in this book, you will learn who taught me how to authentically love others. The answer may surprise you!

I grew up in Ferndale, just outside of Baltimore, along with my brother, who was four years older than me. Raymond was five feet eleven in the fifth grade. Me? I am still only five feet six inches tall. For most of my life, I wanted desperately to receive some respect from my dad and my brother, thinking my size was the problem. As I would learn much later in life, my dad had a misplaced honor system about people overall and saw women as almost second class to him.

The largest differences between the treatment of Ray (my brother) and me by my dad was on the sports field. My brother was a gifted athlete. He was big for his age and did well in sports, which pleased my dad. As a short person, I did not have the sports skill that my dad respected. Looking back at my childhood, many patterns emerged growing up that would serve me well later in life, but at the time, as a young person, I simply resented how life was transpiring within my family.

Many weekends after the work around the house was done, the family went out to my "uncle Johnny's shore house." I think sometimes my dad envied his brother's wealth. Dad's chase after wealth placed a lot of stress on their marriage. Even as a pre-teen, I did not notice the financial issues that would later cause catastrophic damage to their marriage.

There was a lot of anger that developed between my mom and dad over finances. Of course, I heard their fights, but I figured all married couples fought like they did. My dad decided to go to Florida for different working arrangements and move us there a few months later. It became obvious that my mom did not agree with some of the financial decisions dad made, which would eventually split the family. This resentment would soon escalate, and their fights were open for even our neighbors to see and hear by the time we were in Florida.

One of the most vivid bad memories concerning their severe disagreements was watching mom behind the wheel of our black car while dad hollered at her with both hands on the front hood, as though he could stop her from moving. I remember with horror, wondering as this scene unfolded, if I was going to witness a funeral or a divorce.

A year after moving from Maryland to Florida, my mom and dad divorced. I was thirteen at the time. They had only been married eighteen years. Their divorce was very predictable, as I remember several years of intense fighting, disrespectful name-calling, and constant badgering of each other. In the years that followed that horrific time in my life, my dad re-married six more times and lived with a few other women as well. The last person he spent his life with was a wonderful lady who thought the world of him, although they did argue and fuss continually. My mom married two more times and then spent her last thirty years single, which seemed to comfortably suit her.

After their divorce, I lived with my mom and my brother through junior and senior high school. I learned many life lessons watching my mom struggle through hardships that would have stopped most people. At one point, she worked three jobs and earned her bachelor's degree in five years because a supervisor told her she could not teach the students in her cafeteria where she was the manager. Then, at the age of 63, she earned her master's degree. Remember that she was forced to leave junior high school as a young woman, so she had come a long way in her life.

My mom was a great influence on me in many areas of my life. However, learning how to develop a wholesome marriage was not one of those areas. As I grew up, I determined to make my marriage much better than the one my parents had, but I did not have a plan to build on just yet. That methodology was closer than I could imagine, and it came to me in a very curious fashion over the next several years, even before I met Elaine.

My folks were not in any way "religious" as I grew up. They were more closely "anti-religious." I did learn a devotion to other people in general from them. On numerous occasions, before and after their divorce, I witnessed genuine service extended to people in our neighborhood who had even less than us. It is a shame that they never learned how to direct that kindness towards each other. Admittedly, I received many mixed messages through the years from my parents. A girl I dated in high school would provide my spiritual training. I also saw, from some of the couples in her church, a glimpse of how a husband and wife could successfully work through difficulties to create a peaceful relationship in spite of life's hardships.

You do not need to walk in your family's legacy

Can you see from these thumbnail sketches that Elaine and I grew up in extremely different family upbringings? Creating a great marriage became a huge priority for me, since I did not learn how to be a caring husband from my childhood background. Although I was not raised with a spiritual or a church background, I still wanted to have a solid marriage. In the next chapter, I will share a bit more about how I was "encouraged" to go to Bible class and eventually became a Christian. As I mentioned in the previous paragraph, it was at that church where I discovered some remarkable truths about being a good husband.

It dawned on me that the best way to learn how to become a great husband was to "pick" someone's mind personally or learn through books or also watch how good married couples treated each other. Marriage enrichment became a passion from these early seeds of desire.

Fast Forward to Oklahoma where I met the Girl for me

Even before Elaine and I got married, as an engaged couple at college in Oklahoma, we studied together what a Christian home looked like. At college, we studied a course together called, "The Christian Home." We worked through the homework assignments and classroom lectures together. In that class, it became much clearer that we had extremely different views about life. I thought at the time it was solely because of our drastically different upbringings and we could easily work out any issues. Boy how naive I was! My past had clouded my understanding that background differences, and also male and female elements, created how a couple views life situations. As we transitioned from engagement into marriage, I saw even more puzzling questions arise, which I did not know to handle. I truthfully felt that any two Christians could work out tedious situations that arose if they trusted God strong enough. By the way, on the surface that is good doctrine. However, the key is to be focused on being obedient to each other and submit unconditionally to God.

What lay in store for us was some big hurdles to leap over as a newly married couple. Six months after we met, we got married. This is not a recommendation for other couples to imitate, it just happened that way for us. This first year of marriage for us was made more difficult since I became the full-time preacher for a small church, a job I was ill equipped to fulfill. They needed a preacher, and I needed a job. It was a disaster on many fronts. Our marriage took several "hits" that first year. However, on a positive note, since my first preaching job was in Elaine's home town, I did get the opportunity to see how her family interacted with each other, which was a blessing.

After one year of marriage, we moved from Michigan to North Carolina for ten months and then on to Louisiana, where I spent two years studying to become a better preacher, more qualified to do the work of an evangelist. While in school, we were gifted with another opportunity for personal growth, our first child. I have enjoyed each stage of personal development along the way, although at times, I wondered if God was not simply blessing us way beyond our reach!

The quest to create a great marriage stayed in the forefront of my mind all through preacher training and our first ministries that followed. A "revelation" of sorts occurred to me through this journey, that you do not "find your passion in life, it surfaces through life experiences." You will discover your true passion through life experiences. A person can focus on and intentionally polish their skills, but whatever their fixation is, it will surface very clearly for them. Some people develop very tightly focused niches, but it grows out of a heartfelt desire to spend their free time in a certain activity. Helping couples become the close-knit pair that they were created to be, is my passion.

As a couple, we read many types of marriage books, attended marriage seminars, and observed other couples whom we respected and wanted to learn secrets from. When our life settled in a bit after our third child was born and I was back on track with preaching, personal marriage enrichment became a serious subject that consumed many hours of my study. This focused expedition to better understand my wife became like an obsession. After being married over thirteen years, I was discouraged that I still did not have all the answers about her.

Learning to become a better husband

For at least ten more years, we invested heavily into marriage and marriage-related themes for our learning process. As a couple, we studied books and watched videos (before DVDs and Blu-ray) about marriage relationships and even became facilitators for one person's marriage seminars.

So what does a person do with all this acquired information? I was learning a lot about my wife and soon discovered a similarity between her and other wives, which other husbands could benefit from knowing. We developed a two-day marriage seminar, limited to less than twenty couples. There has been tremendous growth among the attending couples who applied the principals transferred to them through the materials presented.

The initial purpose for conducting the seminars was to help couples go from good to great in their particular marriage. These weekend sessions were not an attempt to keep a couple out of divorce court. However, we found that several marriages were in critical danger of falling apart, with no one outside that particular marriage realizing the mess this couple had in their lives. When the struggling couple applied these new principles to their marriage, these key concepts could reverse the negative trends that threatened their relationship. If only one partner was fully committed to working at their marriage, they didn't always work. If both husband and wife applied these concepts, the damage was repaired more quickly. This became an amazing way to see, in a real-world setting, just how uniquely different men and women really are.

We were not able or equipped to deal with any abuse, either physical or emotional. Any person who is in an abusive situation must take immediate action through professional channels to resolve these serious issues.

Husbands: this book will help your marriage!

Those seminars led to the birth of this book. This book reveals many areas where a married couple will nurture their intimacy. A marriage brings together two people, from different backgrounds and life experiences. How a particular marriage grows or deteriorates will depend upon the husband and wife's personal growth and commitment to each other. This book can help in your marriage journey.

Within these pages, you will discover helpful suggestions to increase communication and develop a closer relationship. Do not allow past family problems to become the standard for a marriage in the future. Individual childhood traditions can be used to strengthen the present marriage bond if a husband is willing to do some "homework."

Learning how to romance a wife is a joyful experience. Despite our extreme differences, we made our marriage of forty years a solid example for other couples to witness. Positively shaping and creating a good, lasting marriage is a learned experience. All marriages are in the process of continuous instability, so tender care is always necessary. The changes in our relationship came gradually, through several stages of marriage, by applying sound procedures to our relationship.

Looking back through forty years, God's handiwork and nudges are evident, as people and circumstances opened up to teach lessons about His design for a man and a woman to form this entity called a marriage. The Bible gives good insights for forming a Christian home. It is illuminating to see those lessons in the flesh through godly couples working to honor His designs in action.

Corrective changes to a marriage can be accomplished when the life partners choose to serve each other. This first chapter is to nudge a couple, specifically the husband, in the right direction towards creating an enjoyable marriage. At the end of each chapter notice these "**PEP PILLS**"; which are suggestions to demonstrate positive affirmations from the husband to his wife, which also encourages open communication.

Here is where "the rubber meets the road," the right type of marriage "PEP PILLS" for you:

Here are some preliminary thoughts about these exercises:

1. Do not make these exercises too drawn out. Keep them simple and fun.
2. By the end of the book, you will have some great ideas to continually romance your bride!
3. Perhaps keep a separate notebook or create a document on the computer where these ideas can be stored.
4. After finishing a particular chapter, think of new ideas that fit, and come back and list those new ideas for later use.
5. Build a personal library of creative ideas to woo your wife for the next 60 or 70 years.

"PEP PILLS" FOR YOUR MARRIAGE -

Action Steps To A Better Marriage Relationship

#1 What are four reasons you can list on a page that says you believe you married the right woman? You might say something like "I knew I married the right person because . . ." or "when I . . . (your idea) " After you list these ideas on a piece of paper or in your phone or planner, jot them down on individual pieces of post-it notes, and leave one per day with a few days in between. Maybe put a heart or a smiley face on the post-it note along with your thoughts. The idea is that, since you have her as queen of your heart, now just tell her so. Stick these notes somewhere she will find them easily. Be sure you notice what she does with these notes. You might see that she keeps them prominently posted for others to see.

When I did this exercise, I came up with eight reasons fairly quickly that I knew I married the right person. (Elaine stuck hers on the kitchen cabinet doors.) A couple of these were very basic like: "She is a good mother and grandmother," and, "I saw how much she wanted to be a great preacher's wife." Does this help your situation? Look at her in the unique fashion that only you can. You two share your life together. If you need some help, email me!

#2 Search in her "space" (her office or some part of the house where she does her hobbies) to see how you can do little favors for her that does not disturb her environment, which she may not notice for a while. It is OK if she does not readily observe your assistance, since her sub-conscience is picking up on the changes. You know what I mean about this, right? It is just like when your "radar" goes off and you can't quite put your finger on it but you know something is changed. You look back at this area and notice that something has been moved or a tool is not where you left it.

I noticed that her wastebasket had been missed a few times. I picked up the pieces of paper. I am on the lookout for a few more chores I can help her with.

#3 Start Small But Be Consistent In Devotion To Her

Listen fellows, her sensitivity is much greater than yours in many areas. Your wife will see that something positive has happened and may not know precisely what it is at first. Start doing little activities before she asks you to do them and without looking for something in return. These actions will make her day a bit easier. Try some of these activities for your wife.

- Pick up all the pieces of paper around her wastebasket.

- Make sure the dirty laundry is in the basket and not on the floor.

- If her computer needs some upgrading, get to it without being asked to do it.

- Clean off the dinner table cheerfully.

- Load the dishes into the dishwasher.

- If the laundry needs changing from the washer to the dryer, change it for her.

- Take over in the evening so she can have a "mom's night off," and encourage her to enjoy herself – encourage her to take a bath in quietness, or perhaps put her feet up and read or surf the net. Whatever she enjoys doing, create an atmosphere of relaxation for her.

- Pick up the toys if you have children. (Be sure you are not leaving your stuff out so she has to pick up after you.)

- Be ready to eat when the food is ready.

- Encourage her at every venture: is she starting a new diet? home organizing? a new class? Find a way to let her know you are her greatest cheerleader. Be cautious, but be very supportive.

- NOTE: If it is not your normal action to compliment your wife, she may at first look for your hidden agenda, so find ways give her lavish praise. After awhile, she will understand that you really have her best interest in mind. Consistent sincere praise will win in the end.

Have some fun, and see how secretive you can be in these works. How often can you complete these bits of kindness without her even noticing they are happening? Remember that love functions sacrificially. Try some of these suggestions, and create a personal list as well. Husbands seem to work well from lists, so go ahead and make a few great lists to encourage your bride. Wherever important lists are stored, create these reminders in a unique fashion to keep these lists ready for action?

Share any extra activities with me at the email listed in the front of the book so we can pass the suggestions around a bit to other husbands.

Always expect the best in Your Marriage!

CHAPTER 2

This Crazy Thing Called Love

What is functional love between a husband and wife? How is love obtained? And perhaps even more importantly, how do you learn to express genuine love to your wife?

For most of my early life, I did not realize what genuine "love in action" looked like, especially as it pertains to a married couple. I told you in Chapter One that my parents were at odds with each other fairly often. Since this was my reality, I figured every home functioned that way. My friends' folks argued like mine, so I thought that was the natural way a married couple behaved. When I was eventually shown what genuine, authentic love looked like, I was deeply touched. Many people have contributed to my interest in developing authentic love in my relationships. Sometime during my junior or senior year in high school, I began to witness genuine love in action. Genuine love doesn't just happen between romantic partners or between husbands and wives and takes many forms, as we will discover below. My observance of genuine love started between ladies in the church early on in my walk with the Lord, and then I saw it unfold between men who showed genuine concern for each other. It is a part of my makeup that I observe people. They facinate me. It is easy to identify a phony hug or made up cheek kiss but here there was something else to these folks. It was something missing in me and I wanted to have some of it, whatever "It" was!

At first, it was as though I stood on the sideline and observed these relationships from the outside, with my former style of life surrounding me as well. I noticed ladies talking about each other's children as if they were a connected family who had grown up together. Understand that the reason this was foreign to me was these folks were not biological sisters. They just went to church together. At least that is how it ran in my mind. They would laugh at situations where one child got into a situation with food or mud and then another chimed in how their little boy did the same thing just the other day. They made plans to be together that week or the next to talk and study a bit. These women enjoyed being together and it was not just in a church pew! My observations went outside the regular services.

In a short while I was invited to participate as one of the members of the congregation in many activities and not simply the Sunday services. Several families invited me to their house for meals and to just hang out with some of the other teens. There was a genuine concern for other members who shared more than food together, they shared their daily troubles or successes and worked on several projects that other members needed help to accomplish. Several teens were invited go along and help. Because of past "volunteering" by my dad I figured these men just needed some unskilled labor to do the dirty stuff. That was a completely wrong impression. They did more of the dirty jobs and showed us how to perform some of the skilled jobs. Later I would learn these guys wanted us along to mentor us in serving others. This was really a radical new concept to me!

Here were men listened to each other, prayed for each other, laughed together and calle each other "brother". It was not a show for my benefit either. It was men who were closer than a group of "bowling buddies" or some other external social interaction which drew them together which really enjoyed being together. They had a genuine concern for each other's welfare.

These simultaneous situations between people allowed me to witness what a distinct difference can occur between people. Since some actions were of genuine love and respect towards each other and this was not my normal lifestyle, I did not recognize it at first for what it truly was. It would take a while for this authentic love to become real for me. Life style patterns take a long time to change even when we see better examples right in front of our eyes.

LOVE – GENUINE OR FAKE?

When I first started watching true love flow between people, I thought it was fake. I had seen my parents and other grownups act one way around their family and of course a completely different way in public. This was hypocrisy, yet most folks seem to naturally demonstrate this behavior, depending upon the circumstances, believing that it is acceptable behavior. While they were still married, I remember a few times where my mom and dad were having a heated argument where dad's face would get red or mom would be flailing her arms and walking abut quickly all the while they squabbled about some petty issues, and the phone would ring. One of them would storm over to the phone and whoever answered the phone went from yelling at the other spouse a few seconds earlier or hollering at one of us kids to a very peaceful "hello?" when they answered the phone. Because this happened often – when they answered the phone, or went to the front door if someone knocked, or after we departed the car after a family skirmish when we went for a visit – I thought it was the norm between people who said they loved each other.

To realize how deep seated a learned behavior can become, I would catch myself practicing this behavior more times than I want to admit in our marriage. Too often I tried to "solve" differences between Elaine and myself by shouting or using intimidation to get my way. The truly sad part is that thes situations were not restricted to weekdays as I blew up at the kids or Elaine shortly after preaching some sermon about the merits of Jesus loving us. The problem is certainly not with the Bibles instructoins on love. It is with our life misapplications.

Our children can attest to my setbacks in this area of my parenting. Sorry kids! Since I had witnessed this continous destructive behavior growing up it would take a while to become a valid method of acceptable behaviorin my life. Anger and emotional bullying was the pattern in my life until it dawned on me that was not how a husband should actively love his wife. It took a while of noticing these wonderful differences in my role models before and during our marriage before my reactions for negative life issues would change in my life. These negative patterns go on in may marriages to a greater or lesser degree than it did in ours.

This negative treatment of one spouse towards the other can spring out of a person's "reality" from their childhood learned conduct. To change any lifestyle, a person has to recognize the bad conduct and then create a determination to change those bad manners. They can transform from a negative life pattern to develop a positive life pattern. This requires an observance of a good behavior pattern and then a determined discipline to act in a better fashion. Change is always slow. Our culture sends mixed messages to men and women, concerning the value or the definition for love. A quick glance at the world will illustrate that most folks today don't seem to know what true love in action actually looks like. Mixed messages abound to confuse children. To express the different ways this word love is used in our culture, notice a few practical illustrations that contribute to this confusion, at least for men.

WHAT DID SHE JUST SAY?

You have no doubt heard women say, "Oh I just love that purse!" (or shoes, hat, dress, earrings, etc.). To a man, those words may have seemed strange or perhaps even insincere. Comedians like Jeff Foxworthy have become wealthy by touting the extreme differences between how men and women express themselves over various items. Jeff speaks about how one hunter, all dressed up for a day in his tree stand, wouldn't say to his hunting buddy, "Hey Jim, I just love your boots!" Men do not use the word "love" to express appreciation for an inanimate object or for how some other man looks in his clothes. Because of this, it strikes men as strange when a woman says to another woman, "I just love your hat." and in the next instance looks at her husband all dreamy eyed and says, "I love you!" That sends a mixed message to men who do not comprehend the difference women make over these two concerns. Men wonder which love is real and which one is fake.

The problem is compounded for men, as women are **not** being fake in either situation. But men do not perceive this dialogue as their women being very authentic until they learn to better understand a woman's thought processes. Just listen to some young girls playing, and notice the same messages often being exchanged between the girls. Females are "wired" this way. However, men have to learn how to express genuine, authentic love. So how do men learn what "Authentic Practical Love" truly is? Let's see what true love is and how it has been expressed down through time. The early Greek language can help us distinguish between the similarities and differences in the usage of this word "love".

LET ME SHARE BRIEFLY "LOVE" FROM THE GREEK LANGUAGE

In the first century, when Jesus was on the earth, the Greek language spoken by most people was more precise than our present day English. To give an example of its precision, they had four words to express the one English the word "love." A very **brief** definition for each of these four words might help to better understand the dynamics of this English word "love".

Eros – This means erotic love, human emotions generated through sexual stimulation. It is not used in the Bible. It is where the term "erotic" comes from.

Storge– The love a parent has for a child. It is the unconditional emotion a mother, has which begins inside the womb. It is not dependent upon what a child does.

Phileo – also "philadelphia," or brotherly love; friendship developed between two persons.

Agape – the highest form of devotion and service to another. This is completely beyond emotion. Jesus said to "love our enemies." This would be impossible if He used any of the other words of "love," as they have some emotion guiding their behavior. It would become an oxymoron to try to "phileo" our enemy.

This is not to present a language lesson in the differences between Greek and English, except to show that, even in the Bible, knowing what a person is actually saying makes a huge difference in understanding a passage of scripture. Is the word used in a particular passage of scripture about a parent, a friend, or someone who is my enemy? If a person is told to love this person, which Greek word is being applied? It can be extremely effective to see how a husband is to love his wife. Is it as a friend or unconditional submission to her needs?

So, now back to our discussion on "What is practical love between a husband and his wife?" How can men, really learn to love their wife as told to by the apostle Paul in *Ephesians* 5:25–33? Paul says in verse 25,"Husbands, love your wives, just as Christ also loved the church and gave Himself up for her," And in verse 28 "So husbands ought also to love their own wives as their own bodies. He who loves his own wife loves himself." The really interesting one is verse 33 where Paul shows the different needs for the husband and the wife, "Nevertheless, each individual among you is to love his own wife even as himself, and the wife must see to it that she respects her husband." (New American Standard Version 1997) Women need love and men need respect. Men have to learn what love really is all about.

What type of love is Paul referring to? This word "love" is agape, the self-sacrificing series of actions focused on a wife's best interest. Husbands are told several times in the Bible to "love your wife." Therefore, this form or type of "love" is a learned experience for men. Since men are not programmed to love (agape) their wife internally, how are they to accomplish this directive? Learning how a husband must accurately love his wife is the specific purpose of this chapter.

LET ME SEE THIS *THING* FOR A MINUTE

For men, the "agape" love must come through an education process either from their parents or from some other mentor. Men need to gain this knowledge through several sources. First, they need to hear what genuine love for their life. Next they need to observe real-life actions of manly service, modeled by someone who can impact their life before they will accept it. Agape is something that is a learned experience for men, modeled and transferred from one man to another. Women do not need this knowledge, as they understand it naturally. Therefore, this is a difficult lesson for men to learn from women because their gender views for this concept are so different. It is possible for a man to witness authentic love by a woman. However, it may take a man some time to fully comprehend this active service. Men do understand sincere friendship, but genuine "agape" is a new toy for a male's experimentation. Because husbands need to learn about love (agape) to fully treat their wives properly, let's explain this mystical thought with a few helpful illustrations before it is applied to a marriage.

How Is love a straight line and not circular?

Person "A" **to** person "B"   www.pixabay.com

Agape is a straight-line action from one person to another without any reciprocation desired from the person receiving the agape to the person extending the devoted kindness. There is no "hidden agenda" in authentic agape love. On a battlefield, one soldier is willing to lay down his life for a stranger in the same uniform. This action is agape in real time, as the men might not have known each other, so they certainly do not have any emotional attachment towards one another. That is how a person can authentically "love his enemy." There is no good relationship built up between the two persons. Actually, from one side of the equation, one person is actively seeking to do harm to the other. True love seeks to do good for the person one is showing love to. Agape is an active motivator, which seeks to do what is best for the other person without regard for one's own personal needs being fulfilled.

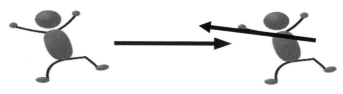

www.pixabay.com

On the other hand, philadelphia/love, is a reciprocal arrangement built upon shared experiences and generally happens when two persons have compatible personality traits. Once a person knows a fellow soldier, he might lay his life down for that soldier because they are friends. This action of "philadelphia" is what genuine friendship between two or more people looks like. It makes no difference which gender is a friend. Philadelphia is a give-and-take arrangement, where two or more persons develop a close bond because of similar likes and dislikes. A husband and a wife should develop this type of love for one another.

To set these words in a practical arena, agape is extended out from the source to another person who is typically unable to respond in kind. Agape does not expect any return on its investment. Agape is **not** emotionally driven, as is philadelphia. Agape is what happens when a person serves another person in a "soup kitchen" or "food bank." The server does not expect the person receiving the food to give anything back. The server is there to serve the person's need for a meal. On the other hand, if two friends go to a restaurant together, one person may pay for both meals because of their friendship: "philadelphia" in action. This payment may not be because it was one friend's "turn"; it may be just because they felt the desire.

Sometimes agape is learned from children who are not trying to be manipulative. They just want to express their concern for another person as they seek the other person's highest good. The tragic problem in society is that children are too often trained to become selfish and squash this genuine service toward others. I did not grow up in an environment for learning "agape love"; therefore, as a young adult, I had to discover how it looked in action. Let me tell you how I became skilled at agape and how I have been transformed by its marvelous power through several unexpected sources. If you are reading this book because you need to inject actual, self-giving love into your marriage, read on – there is hope, no matter your background!

HOW DOES A MAN *CRACK* THIS "LOVE" (AGAPE) CODE?

Two different sources cracked the code for genuine (agape) love in my life. I learned what authentic love in action looked like first through the church which started in high school and then through my lovely wife. The church prepared me to receive the unconditional love I would receive from my wife. My church "experience" spans many years and three continents. For brevity, I will only mention a few of the high points of my learning experience.

While in high school, the mother of one girl I dated became very special to me and made a great impression upon my life. This woman taught me about Jesus, as well as the core function of the church. She also showed what unconditional love means. I am eternally grateful for her unreserved love, long before I was able to give much back to her or to the church. Of course, she did not show love to get anything in return. Margret, my girlfriend's mom, taught me what love does, as she was concerned for my soul and spent many hours teaching me the Bible. This wonderful person led me as far as she could and then "handed" me off to others who would continue my spiritual education. She did this because she was concerned for my welfare and not for her personal satisfaction. The members of that church in St. Petersburg, Florida, especially Charlie and Elizabeth Haslem and Gayle Crow (the preacher), showed me how to study God's Word and to become a leader for God's kingdom. On several occasions, Charlie chastised me to not let my emotions overrun my brain. Here was a man who showed true love to someone who was not going to return love in the same manner as it was extended. Many times he showed me "tough love" for my needed maturity. His wife, Elizabeth, drove home a powerful point about being my best by stating a beautiful phrase repeatedly: "What you are is God's gift to you. What **you become** is your gift to God!"

> "What you are is God's gift to you.
>
> What **you become** is your gift to God!"

These folks had a beautiful effect on my life as a young Christian struggling through so many emotional issues. At that time, it was not apparent that they were developing in me a desire to practice mature, unconditional love towards others. I could write another entire book (I might just do that!) about the total manifestation of love in action verified by these folks. The life lessons from there had a profound impact upon my life. They watched over me even when I went off to Germany with the US Air Force. I did not realize that Gayle had contacted the local English-speaking missionary near my base in Germany, Trent Campbell.

The next couple to greatly influence my life would be Trent & Billie Campbell, the minister and his wife. They did many selfless actions of generosity not immediately seen by the recipients of their love, including me. The first act of love from Trent was to contact me within a few weeks of being on a foreign land without any friends besides those in the Air Force. I learned quickly that the church and especially the Campbell's were genuine friends indeed.

Many times, I would drop by to visit them or I would get a phone call where Trent would ask, "Have you eaten dinner yet?" No matter my answer, he would say, "Come on down we were just getting ready to order a pizza!" He would then ask about some of the other members of the church at the Air Base or my fellow airmen at the barracks, and I would round them up and we went to supper at the Campbell's house. After a while, we caught on to Trent's message, since they had already eaten, but he wanted to create a reason for us to get together. We spent many hours just chatting about our lives or about a passage in the Bible that Trent would "throw out there" for us to discuss. It was in these sessions that I saw the Campbell's showing genuine and unconditional love for us. This was never "preachy" or put-on stuff. They just served us in a genuine fashion that still touches my heart almost fifty years later. As I grew spiritually, I worked to give back to these Christians by paying it forward to others who needed to learn about authentic love. It did not occur to me at the time, but because of these early events, I was being groomed for a wonderful awakening a short time later.

I DID NOT SEE THAT COMING

After my brother died, while I was on temporary duty in Turkey, I was discharged from the Air Force and went back to my home in St. Petersburg, where I led a different role in the church as a leader for the young people and met a brother named Mike LeVasseur. Mike would help me in ways that reached far beyond our friendship. Mike and I took the young people to various events, helping them understand what true love looked like as we served their spiritual needs and helped them understand how to cope with life's situations. Mike was a good servant for the young people to observe, and so I also observed love in action from this brother.

Mike decided to go to Oklahoma Christian College and invited me to join him on the trip. I said, "Sure, why not?" and was planning to come back to Florida after a short visit to Oklahoma, where we stayed with some mutual friends. As it turned out, I was encouraged to stay as a student by our friend, who was a professor there. This small, insignificant decision would alter my life in a positive and dramatic way, which I could not have envisioned when Mike invited me to travel with him to Oklahoma.

There in Oklahoma, after three months, I met Elaine. It was a night where many of the students were playing a group game called "Wink" or "Killer" (depending on whom you asked). The object of the game was to find the "killer" who knocked off the other persons sitting in the big circle by winking at them, which was the way you were killed. You each had a card, face down in front of you, which showed that you were still alive. When the "killer" winked at you, you had to turn your card over showing that you had been eliminated. I explain the game because while playing this game this one cute, curly-headed, blonde girl, who could not wink without scrunching up her whole face, became extremely fascinating to me. As I listened to her a bit more, I took a strong liking to her, and I wanted to get to know her much better. Her "date" that night was a good friend of mine, Steve, so when I asked if they were formally "dating," he said, "No, would you like to date her?" Of course, I said "Yes!" and so it was arranged through a couple of phone calls from Steve to Elaine and then from me to Elaine. We went on our first date the next day to the small church where I was preaching, and six months to the day we met, we were married. She caught me with her special "wink" and so much more! The story gets much better.

SO GLAD FOR HER WINK!

My precious bride and I have been married forty years, this April (2014), and it has been a wonderful trip. More than any other single person, Elaine has taught me the practical meaning of agape love. In the previous chapter, you saw how her parents demonstrated love to her. Her mom characterized genuine servant hood to her family, to her neighbors, and actually to any person she ever met.

Elaine wanted to marry a preacher, and God honored that request. As He often does, there was more in the life experiences extended to her than she had prayed for. I have seen Elaine develop into a more self-assured woman, who is an excellent role model to many of the women in our church, to our community, to our children, and to our grandchildren. Many ladies seek her advice and counsel about their marriage and life in general. My bride has been a terrific role model for our children, teaching them to demonstrate authentic love unashamedly to their family or friends. I have also learned new depths about love through my children.

YOU DO NOT NEED TO LIVE YOUR FAMILY LEGACY FROM YOUR CHILDHOOD

How would I characterize the active love expressed by Elaine and our three children? Open, unimpeded bursts of affection capped off by sincere vocal statements of, "I love You!" Without formally telling our children, "You HAVE TO tell them you love them," Elaine taught our children how to boldly show love for others. All three of our children *always* say "love you!" as their way to end our conversations. It is the natural way they conclude most of their conversations. Authentic love has so permeated our conversations that I have to be wary when I am discussing business or speaking with some new person I just met that I don't blurt out "love you!" when I am finishing a dialogue with them. My grandkids say it as a matter of fact, "love you granddad!" Looking back on my childhood, I do not recall hearing those words, and I did not see love in action. Remember, you do not have to live your childhood legacy. You can change your family heritage.

SO, WHAT'S LOVE GOT TO DO WITH IT?

Many generations after me will know what true love is because my wife taught through her life what true love in action looks like. It is more than the words; it is the true service to others. Thanks to her mom and dad instilling in her family this trait of unconditional affection for each other, my grandchildren always give me a big hug and honestly tell me "love you granddad!" which of course creates a huge lump in my throat.

Succeeding generations will be undeniably impacted due to simple honest actions practiced today. I did not learn to understand how to really act in genuine love until it became visible in someone else's life, such as the Haslem's, the Campbell's, and many of my friends who showed me unconditional love. When I met Elaine, I discovered how to give back this love that had transformed my life. My children continue to blast me daily with the words and expressions that have altered my life for the better. In essence, my children have been a reflection of love from their mother, and they have penetrated my heart with their goodness. I know that my generational legacy is already better than the one I grew up knowing. How much better depends on my children continuing to train the next generation, to train the next generation, and so on. Through open, honest communication with my wife, we still learn more about agape, and we then teach others how to experience this genuine agape in their marriage.

Husbands, love your wife. This is a learned experience for men. The great news is that a husband can learn how to show his wife the complete unconditional agape that she craves in her core. Why would a husband hold back what his wife was designed to receive? Husband, love your wife.

In the next chapter learn how to make intimate communication a pleasing practical experience.

"PEP PILLS" for your marriage -
Action Steps To A Better Marriage Relationship

HAVE FUN WITH THESE *"PEP PILLS"*

CHAPTER 2 : PEP PILLS = Here are some actions that will stimulate practical love in action. These will identify your wife's definition and application of "AGAPE." Seek to express to her techniques she understands of what true love looks like in her own language. As husbands, continually learn to reflect back to your wife the love she naturally shows towards others. This book is written to teach husbands procedures about how to love their wives. These PEP PILLS are designed so a husband can become a better student of his wife to provide her the love she craves.

 # 1 - PEP PILL - Tell your wife *seven* extra times EVERY DAY for at least the next two months, that you love her. This should be at times that you would not regularly tell her. For instance, stop whatever is happening right now and go tell her you love her. If she happens to ask, "What was that for?" You could answer, "because you need to know how much you mean to me!" or "because I wanted to!" or something that expresses these emotions to her. This doesn't have to always be in person; it could be by phone, text, email, or a note on the fridge – in whatever ways you two communicate.

Make a game of it to find atypical times and methods to verbally tell her that you love **_HER_** (for example, leaving "I love you" messages for her in unexpected and surprising places).

 # 2 - PEP PILL - Cuddle with no hidden agenda. Cuddle with your wife every single day. Women are very approachable for snuggling, and it helps them to see that you care about them. Make the special effort to cuddle for no extra reason than you just want to be near your wife. If needed, go hug her for an extended amount of time. A hug is a standing cuddle to her.

 # 3 - PEP PILL - Do what many husbands do not do for their wives: *remember those unique dates.* Do you remember her birthday? How about your wedding anniversary? Why is so much written about these events from a negative perspective about husbands? It is because many husbands do not treat these days as being very special events in a husband's mind. Even if these and other certain days are not special to you, most likely they hold precious memories for your wife. In order to let her know how important she is to you, remember to celebrate her special dates.

So, here is how to score extra points for yourself as to special dates that your wife holds near and dear to her:

Make a list of any date that your wife sees as significant and put them on your calendar or add a reminder on your phone or computer. Does she remember the date you met? Your first kiss? How about where you went on your first anniversary? When is her birthday? Be sure you do something special for her special days.

As an extra treat, send her a card a week early about your anniversary. Be sure to write in the "early card" that you know your anniversary is in a week, but you want her to know you are already thinking about it, since it is special for you as well.

Do you want to "score" even more extra points? Always send your mother-in-law and your mother a birthday card without your wife knowing you did it. Just get these precious ladies an appropriate card and send it. Your wife will hear about it through these other sources. Just make it seem as though there is nothing to it.

Wives want to be treated in a special fashion from their husbands. Remembering her special dates can assist you in this fashion.

Always expect the best in your marriage!

CHAPTER 3

Verbal Communication can be like a "bull in a china closet,"

What Is Practical, Verbal Communication?

Communication is necessary for two or more people navigate through the most precious areas of life to attain peace where turmoil previously existed. It is to exchange ideas so that two people understand each other's words and motives behind those ideas. Allow me to share some early confusions I had when it came to verbal communication and show you how to handle problems in a marriage with open, honest communication. While the strict definition for communication covers several varieties of informational interchanges, verbal and non-verbal, this chapter is primarily focused on **Verbal Communication between a husband and his wife**. Verbal Communication can be like a "bull in a china closet," or it can be the ability to effectively exchange any idea you want with your wife in a peaceful quiet manner.

The basis for this chapter is not simply about communication *techniques.* It is to assist a husband in communicating in an effective manner with his wife. Let's tear down any barriers that exist and shed those unwanted or unnecessary habits that dampen effective communication. If difficulty exists in effectively communicating thoughts to his bride, a husband needs to replace negative thoughts with positive actions. If we are brutally honest, people typically revert to what comes naturally when a situation is threatening or is uncomfortable. Bad habits and discomfort are not acceptable techniques to create a peaceful loving environment that produces genuine love for each other.

For much of my life, I was too aggressive as a communicator. Life seemed to be a continual contest, so I believed that if I talked long enough and loud enough, the other person would give in and I would win! This did not encourage close friendships. This excessive chatter actually accomplished the opposite effect. It seems I have always had a deep-seated emotional need to help people. When I am unable to help someone, I feel inadequate, so I attempt to compensate by talking too much. Another mistaken belief I had was thinking that, if I gave an answer quickly to the first part of a person's sentence, they would see that I knew what they needed. Sadly, that did not work either, and many great relationships were ruined in the process. Even though my skills have improved and I have learned how to adjust my needs and listen before I open my mouth, God isn't finished with me. I am still a considerable "work in progress," but fortunately my wife has also not given up on me.

True Communication

Proper communication between a husband and wife is essential for a marriage to grow. Many experts agree that communication is the indispensable solution to solving any problem between two persons. Consider it this way, if a husband can properly express his ideas in a manner that his wife can precisely value what he is expressing, she can handle the issues he wants her to understand. When the husband fully understands what his wife wants him to perceive from her vantage point, he is less likely to get all flustered or jump to inaccurate conclusions. Here is what accurate communication looks like: a husband or wife comfortably expresses ideas to their spouse, who in turn understands their motives, ideas, and intended outcome. If that is the ideal, what is the reality?

Of course, not all conversations between the husband and wife flow in an easily understood manner do they? In real life, many detached issues cause a blurred understanding of personal concepts. On the basic level, men and women do not understand each other's gender differences or particular operating motives. In a very broad stroke, men tend more towards the straightforward characteristics and women are inclined more towards the emotional. This is a generality and not every couple always follows the classic male/female roles. However, the vast majority of folks fall into these wide-ranging modes of expression. This chapter expresses the core manner in which a man or woman deal with information.

You did *what* to your wife?

Let me briefly present a bit of my background as it relates to communication, or to be more honest, the lack of communication that existed early in our marriage. This is how **NOT** to communicate with a wife. I will then show how I achieved effective communication with my wife. The answer for effective communication is easy, once a person knows how to use a workable system.

Effective communication was lacking early in our marriage. Since I had no real role models from my parents as to how to resolve real tension between Elaine and myself, I did what I knew to do at my gut level. While I am not happy to look back on my antics, I really acted in this manner. When we had disagreements, I tried to goad her into an argument. After all, arguing is how you solve difficult issues in a marriage, right? NO! Arguing is not an effective way to communicate, but it was all I knew at that time. Heated disagreements were my heritage so that is what I referred back to as a young husband. In hindsight, I know it was not a kind way to treat my wife. At first I did not recognize that I was trying to injure an "unarmed" person, as she did not know how to argue! It would have been like boxing with her when she had her arms tied down and I just kept punching her in the face. Not a pretty picture is it?

I have since learned that Elaine does not know how to fight or argue. When I first realized her limitation in this area, I tried to teach her. Pulling her down to my level of intensity was real work. She refused to learn how to act in such a terrible fashion, and so I became frustrated. However, I discovered a huge and valuable lesson along the way. **You cannot effectively argue all by yourself.** You cannot argue against someone who will not argue back at you either. I would shout, talk wildly, raise my voice, and try to get her to open up and fight fair. She would not utter a peep. She simply looked at me with a blank stare, since she did not know why I was assailing her as I did?

I learned a valuable lesson:
You Cannot Argue Against Someone Who Will Not Argue Back At You!

After I calmed down, she would ask me why I got so upset and yelled at her? Now it was my turn to stare with a blank look! In my mind I was thinking, "Because that is how you get your point across!" Sometimes her question would give me an open, and I would charge again. I found out that when the other person does not act like you think they should act, it gets annoying for you. I figured she did not want to understand what I was trying to express because she did not act like a "real" wife. At least that's what I thought? Haven't you seen all those "reliable" TV shows or heard your neighbors going at it like cats and dogs?

Now, I understand there is a better way to get my point across without verbally assaulting my wife. At the beginning of our marriage, I did not know how to address a touchy subject without becoming agitated at her. For many years of our marriage, I did not know how to express my affection to her and my arguing was only one-sided. Somehow, I need to learn a better way.

Communication is not simply using your personal verbal skills.

Another illustration that I had it all wrong was how I let her know I "loved" her. Wait till you read about this!

One particular day, in our first year of marriage, I was trying to show her I loved her by nudging and bumping her repeatedly. After I did this a few times, she looked at me with a strange facial expression and asked, "Why do you do *that*?"

So, I looked a bit rattled and asked her, "What do you mean, *THAT*?"

"Well every time you come past me, you bump me or nudge me with your elbow or you punch me." (Just to set the record straight, these were very gentle nudges and punches, as Elaine will verify.)

"It is because I love you!" I said.

She replied, "No! That's not how I want you to show me you love me."

Actually I felt crushed and bewildered, as I did not know what she meant or what she really wanted me to do.

Growing up, my brother and I always punched and shoved each other. And we loved each other, right? And if you see two brothers anywhere in the same proximity to each other today, they are competing and tussling around. It appears this is the way two brothers show their affection. So, naturally I guessed, "How else was a man supposed to express to his bride how much he loves her?" You jab her or nudge her or tussle with her! I had a steep learning curve when we first got married concerning many area of marriage. Elaine did not understand or remotely appreciate my methods of "endearment" early on in our marriage. I have discovered some marvelous lessons for wholesome, effective communication since then.

If two people can appropriately communicate with each other, they can solve any and all of their relationship problems.

Since the early days of our relationship, I have learned how to convey my love in a more pleasing manner so the information can be cherished. Throughout my marriage journey, I discovered how a person can radically change with skillful training and the correct approach. With smaller marital issues, this information can really enhance the relationship. If there are deep-seated issues from the past ... **GOOD NEWS!** This chapter will create a wonderful relationship between a husband and his wife that is beyond their imagination. A great relationship begins with proper communication. If two people can suitably communicate with each other, they can solve any of their problems. There might be some hidden land mines in that last sentence. What deep-seated problem causes so many divorces in America? Is it finances? Sexual issues? Actually, there is one problem even more damaging than these two.

Notice other marriages; notice that the root issue for any problem the husband and wife are suffering with is pride. Each person in the marriage wants their own way since they believe their way is right. When you dissect arguments about sex, finances, children, or any other situation husbands and wives find themselves entangled, you will see that the root cause is pride. The most heated partner wants something their way. Given time and enough self centered thinking the turmoil gets way out of hand.

However, when a married couple learns to submit to one another, peace is the eventual outcome. This is not to say a couple cannot disagree. Elaine and I do disagree and misunderstand each other, even after forty years together.

However, we do not argue. With the information given about our early years of marriage, understand why I say honestly and upfront, we have only had two actual arguments in our many years of marriage. Only having two actual arguments erupt was not because I did not try to get her to into a verbal fight. Before I learned it is better to effectively communicate I tried to get her to leave her comfort zone and wallow with me in the mud so to speak. My old self prodded her sufficiently during those two times, but despite my best efforts, these additional times did not erupt into arguments. I am not proud of those lapses in judgment; I am just stating the truth. We disagree on issues, and yet we do not argue or fight over any issues. The ironic part to this chapter is that I don't mind doing it her way or making sure she has what she wants in life. It is fascinating, as I look back on our life, that when I sought to meet her needs, I was at peace in our relationship no matter what she wanted. I learned an interesting lesson. It takes two people to become properly inflamed to argue. If only one person is mad, there is no argument. You can't carry on a two sided argument with an inanimate object or a wife who will not be incited by threats. You can discuss different opinions calmly no matter the subject or the separation of opinions.

Do you want to know what is the absolute *secret* to effective communication?

Effective communication is basically very simple: first and foremost, never try to **push your way or ideas** onto the other person. It does not matter who is right or who came up with the idea initially. In your marriage listen to her words with her happiness in mind. If you fully serve your spouse, she will have no reason to fight with you. I learned this concept firsthand from my wife, a woman, as I said, who will not argue. Many examples exist in life about this principle of servant hood. The best example for me was and is Jesus Christ. Since I have seen firsthand that a person can really avoid an argument, I cannot imagine an actual uncontrolled argument between Jesus and anyone else. Jesus did not allow people to coerce Him into acting a certain way they wanted Him to behave. When He was angry in the Temple, He was completely directed

His actions. He was also responding to sinful actions by the people in the Temple. Gandhi or some other peace-seeking person could also be spoken about in this way. Jesus was capable of anger but it was managed completely and not from selfish motives.

I personally do not hold these people in as high a regard as I do Jesus, but they seem to have had their emotions in check much better than I. These other great people had no selfish desire to force their opinions onto other people. They submitted when most of us would boast or focus the spotlight on our self, or they would walk away instead of becoming aggressive. The proverb of "you catch more flies with honey than vinegar" is true. You'll win over more people with acts of kindness than acts of harshness. For a brief moment, think about the gentlest person you know. Why do you have such high regard for that particular quality in them? Is it because of their fiery temper or rude behavior? Of course not. Your respect is due to their complete mental and physical control under extreme tension. Folks who want to argue spend a large amount of effort getting ready for the argument.

Learn to replace the negative with the positive

How do people process information when they are "spoiling for a fight" with someone else? Aren't they focused on collecting the raw data needed to have all the arguments lined up for the best defense of their position to the exclusion of everything else? Don't they ignore what is said in order to focus on a quick rejoinder? Real effort is needed to argue. Learning how to avoid an argument creates a stiff learning curve. It is not easy to alter the base line internal functions that have been so entrenched, but it is workable if someone wants to change. To change emotional patterns is to learn how to correctly express the desired point without inflaming the other person. The only way to do this is to express yourself in a clear and non-angry way.

Learning how to get your point across with kindness is very "manly"; it is not showing weakness it is strength under control. I know, I was tamed on several occasions. I use that word tame in the genuine sense of the word. I do not mean it in a derogatory way. Elaine tamed my temper since I had to negotiate around my initial tendencies to get my point across. In reality, I had to learn how to control my anger to refocus thoughts so she understood what I wanted to get across to her.

This "taming" process is precisely what the word "meek" means. Notice it is **meek, not weak**. A person who is weak does not understand how to apply discipline to their life. But a meek person is alive with true power. The word meek means "strength brought under control." A husband can be absolutely strong and yet be gentle and meek towards his wife. Expressing myself without emotional angry outbursts has been a painful learning experience. Honestly, I like my last years a lot better than I remember our early years of marriage. It is due to learning how to control my temper. I have also learned how to "fight fair" with my wife. Once a person knows the rules, communication can be fun!

Peaceful effective communication was the destination, but how did I get from angry outbursts to where I am today? That is the rest of this chapter, "How does a person learn to effectively communicate with his wife?" In many marriages, it is the wife who can be the wild tempered one and the husband is the person who will not argue. Whoever reads and applies this information can help the other spouse keep from being so aggressive. Here is the rest of the story.

So just how does one change his behavior patterns?

Let's work through this situation one piece at a time. No sort of behavioral change is ever easy nor comfortable. Transformation is a long-term endeavor, not a quick medication, as if a doctor could prescribe: "take two pills to relieve your anger issues." So how does a man actually learn to control their temper or negative frame of mind and, as a result, effectively learn to communicate with his wife? Is it possible that she can value what he wants her to comprehend? Yes, it is doable but the husband has to alter how he approaches a typically harmful situation, especially if his normal reaction is to blow up or lose his temper. Let's begin with some very basic things and work our way up from there.

The key to resolving problems is to ask appropriate key questions and then set a workable course of action or game plan laying out action steps that need to be followed. We will go over several such questions below. This is a simple strategy but not a comfortable solution when emotions get in the way. Fortunately, the results can be quite amazing! **All couples disagree on lots of subjects.** Each day, issues arise that threaten the structure of a marriage. Learning how to handle troubles in a constructive manner is key to achieving a thriving relationship.

Asking good questions can assist in establishing your plan of attack

Fundamental questions and specific action steps along the way determine a workable solution. Keep the end result in mind as we progress through this new learning experience. The end in mind is the answer to the question, "How will he act in a perfect confrontational setting, once he has his emotions absolutely in check?" This "end in mind" provides a person with a reason for working on this journey. Let's begin the questions at that point:

- What is to be ultimately accomplished? What does the finished communication process look like? Do you want to calmly exchange ideas and leave room for her disagreement or input? What topics can be brought up for mutual discussion in a productive manner? What topics are taboo to talk about at this moment? What would it look like if any topic could be added into the conversation and rationally thrashed out without either party getting red faced?

- Is true effective communication between a husband and a wife that important? How signficant is heartfelt dialog? You must decide that a great marriage with open communication at its core is the desired result before any true healing can take place.

- In evaluating my situation, I asked myself, "What did I need to do differently so that Elaine understood what I was trying to get across to her?" Frankly, it took a while to find out what to do to have a different approach than what previously felt comfortable. If learning how to change the approach to a defensive spouse is a goal, there is an ally on your side – ME! I can guide a spouse through the process, but they have to implement these concepts for making intimate communication what it can be. Learn to adapt each action step to fit the personal situation.

So, let's get started shaping the learning process. These guidelines, when applied to a marriage, will change negative outcomes of heated arguments around to dealing with sensitive issues in a constructive fashion. Like any large event, transformation is a gradual process, however, if you continue in the desired direction with proper coaching you can effect marvelous positive modifications.

Having a personal determination that the marriage will become better is the next logical place for effective verbal communication to progress. How committed are you to this endeavor for having great communication between you two? Ask yourself these vital questions and then share the answers with your wife:

- o How is my way working for me now? Are we drawing closer as a couple or becoming more distant?

———————————————————————————

- o Where are we in the various levels of friendly communication?

———————————————————————————

- o Can we really talk about any subject without either of us getting offended or angry because the other partner brought up that particular subject or issue?

———————————————————————————

- o If either of us makes a suggestion, can we openly examine that issue calmly and without any hurt feeling?

———————————————————————————

- o Jot down a few sentences right here that expresses what your communication goals looks like fully developed. Keep in mind that the purpose you seek is to create a great communication process between you two. What does that great communication process look like in your own words? Go ahead and start by writing: I want to have better communication between my wife and me by

_____

_____

_____

_____

_____

_____

_____

o On a scale from one–ten, with ten being the most desirable and one being the least desirable, where do you see your confidential, personal conversations between your wife and you at the present time? If they are not all at a level ten, then there is room for growth. Most couples would see themselves communicating at less than a ten. Write out here what you think your number is at this moment:

_____

Are you doing the "**PEP PILLS**" from chapters one and two so far? If you notice how the book is laid out, it begins at the surface level for a couple's communication process and digs deeper with each chapter. Be sure to implement the "**PEP PILLS**" exercises along the way. It will make this book very practical now and in the years to come. This form of "homework" is there to help any marriage become better for each wife and husband.

"PEP PILLS" for your marriage – Action Steps To A Better Marriage Relationship

HAVE FUN WITH THESE *"PEP PILLS"*

 # 1 - Communicate her words back to her. Use the greatest words to reach any wife's ears – "I Love You!" Do not wait another second. Begin today to **overindulge her** with your verbal unconditional love. Also use every action you can dream up to lavish your wife with unreserved love and honest affection, especially as it relates to your communication skills. These actions are not to get anything in response; they are simply to invest love into her life. I am a grand example of a person who did not know how to effectively communicate with my wife early in our marriage. It takes practice and effort to perfect this language to your bride. She is worth any effort you expend towards her.

Constantly repeating this phrase "I Love You!" can seem insincere, but to your bride, it is better than "music to her ears." These words often strike the tuning fork deep in her soul so grasp her heart gently and tell her often about your love. It is true that most men prefer to be shown high doses of unconditional respect. Women on the other hand, need to be **told** very often that they are loved.

Try this one for size: Tell her "I love you" so many times that she actually warns you to stop saying it to her. Go ahead I dare you! Keep track one day or one week. Can you tell her over 75 times on average per day for a week, "I Love You"? This should be done as a single rifle shot and not as a machine gun.

 # 2 - Questions to open the floodgates for information exchanges. Create some simple open-ended questions to let your wife share some of her inner feelings. Be sure to take some mental notes or perhaps have a notebook ready to jot down her responses to these questions.

For example, starting with some light questions, ask her,

"How would you fill in these sentences":

"Someday I want to . . ."

"A place that would be wonderful to visit would be . . ."

"Something new or adventurous I'd like to try is . . ."

Design a few more light questions to have to ask that relate to your relationship.

Also, ask some deeper thoughts as well (her answers here will give you great insight to your wife's heart):

"What does a perfect marriage look like to you?"

"In this book, I am learning how to communicate better as a husband.

How do you want me to communicate with you more effectively?"

"What habit of mine do you wish I did not have, and why?"

"What are some ways you express your love for me that you think I don't see?"

"What do you believe we need to do to deepen our closeness as a husband and wife?"

"What do I do that makes you feel completely loved?"

Keep in mind that the next chapter will dig a bit deeper into a woman's heart as well.

Always expect the best for your marriage!

CHAPTER 4

Six Secrets for intimate communication for every marriage

It sounds a bit foolish now, but it took me a while to learn that when I raised my voice or outright hollered at Elaine early in our marriage, she would completely shut down. In essence, she became as emotionally protective as a turtle in its shell. No amount of verbal onslaught would open her up. It took many years to understand this dynamic about her. Eventually, I found that tenderly giving her a bit of information, a little at a time, and allowing her to gather it all together created a peace between us. This is not about intelligence. She is very smart. It concerns emotional assurance.

There was a comfort developed when I allowed her to "digest" the information for a later conversation. She could assess the information presented, and we could discuss what we understood about each side of the situation. Because we process information in thoroughly different ways, we learned to present ideas to each other as the other person needed them packaged. It sounds elaborate, but in reality we have formed new habits of approaching each other, so communication is actually quicker these days.

The better equipped a husband is at perceiving his wife's habits and distinctive tendencies, the better he will be at understanding how to capture her heart. Consider these strategies for connecting more intimately with your wife.

These six suggestions are to equip any husband to reach a deeper level of verbal conversation with his wife.

As we begin this section, let me make this disclaimer. If there is actual physical or mental abuse, immediately seek professional help. What I am writing about involves the small skirmishes that are daily irritants we see with married couples that gets under the skin.

Six Secrets To Encourage Intimate Communication

Secret # 1 – Develop within your mind, a "wife-centered intimacy" – isolation is contrary to intimacy.

Secret #2 – Define personal expectations and share them with each other.

Secret # 3 – Defensiveness creates barriers not bridges: learn how to disarm these distrustful barriers

Secret # 4 – Attack the problem and not each other

Secret # 5 – True communication involves repeated forgiveness from both life partners.

Secret # 6 – Develop specialized and discerning listening skills.

So let's dig into these secrets a bit deeper:

Secret # 1 – Develop within your mind, a "wife-centered intimacy" – isolation is contrary to intimacy.

This "wife-centered intimacy" means that she is intentionally enticed to be closer with her husband each day. The wise husband can learn to open himself to his wife's internal needs. When she expresses herself and he acts in a callous manner towards her, he may be seen as insensitive or uncaring. Men come off as being disinterested about their wives since husbands and wives each process data in a different fashion. Whenever he tries to "fix" her problems or whenever he rolls his eyes when she talks about several unconnected actions of her day, he speaks loudly in her language that he does not care about her feelings. **Keep in mind that _feelings_ to a woman are extremely important.** Listen to women speak, and you will hear the word "feel" or its derivative often used. For a man, how he "feels" about some issue may not mean anything at all.

For many wives, verbal communication is the medium for creating and sustaining intimacy. Women use speech to openly bond with their friends. If a man takes note of his wife and her friends' interactions, he will notice they do not exchange ideas for the same reasons as he and his buddies. Verbal interactions are the means by which they deepen their relationships. In the same way, his wife may want to intensify the marriage relationship through spoken communications. Her desire might be to understand her husband, but she also wants to be understood by him as well. She wants him to value her. Active listening is the medium she uses with her friends and desires from her husband.

If a wife asks how her husband's day was, and he cuts her off with a quick, short burst, such as "not much" or "nothing special," she will get the impression he does not care about her or want to let her into his "heart." She takes this process personally. To many husbands, their wives go on about little details that seem to drone on too long for them. That is because she connects through verbal interchanges, which include numerous small details. Her desire may be to bond with him through an exchange of just what happened during the day.

Given that the wife may want to develop a greater intimacy with her husband through verbal exchange, if the husband is verbally distant, it might create dire consequences. Silence is an intimacy killer. The destructive issue is that a wife may not know whom to turn to for the intimacy she craves from her husband.

She may have envisioned, as she grew up, that her husband would value her and meet all her emotional desires. Just sit with her through a few "chick flicks" and watch how the women think about the men in these films. Notice that a lack of close verbal interactions, even in small doses, can cause isolation between a husband and his wife. Work to find common areas to draw each other closer.

Secret # 2 – Define personal expectations and share them with each other.

What was the image of your marriage when the wedding day was approaching? I am not referring to the particulars of the wedding day itself or the honeymoon fun. After the honeymoon ended and the routines started, what pictures came to mind for a real-life marriage?

Do these statements represent some of your early expectations?

- She is the person I want to share my life with.
- Here is the person who is going to make me happy.
- This marriage will be unlike our parents' marriage (or that of some other close relative who was very miserable being married).
- We will have sex every day because we both want each other so desperately.
- Being all alone is a drag, and I finally found that special person to invest in for the rest of my life.
- Together we will work to establish a home that will be a grand example for everyone else to marvel at.
- Jot down a couple of your early expectations

_____

_____

_____

_____

_____

Be honest here. Did expectations meet reality? None of these expectations listed are durable enough to form a strong foundation to last for many years. Take some time to really think through this section and determine what your expectations are for marriage. Take some time to discuss what your various expectations about marriage are and where your marriage is headed?

A married couple needs to know expectations for each other, overall what were they looking to "*GET*" from this covenant arrangement? In their private thoughts, couples enter into their own marriage with a "what's in it for me" attitude. That is not necessarily a bad thought. However, it can be much different from what your spouse is looking for on their "*GET*" list. If both husband and wife pull in the opposite direction, the marriage is stressed and will not last.

Pulling away from each other is a critical problem plaguing any marriage on the verge of separation and divorce. It looks at the arrangement from "me & my" needs and not on the actual focus they vowed at the altar. Any couple in a divorce mentality will speak using many "me" or "I" sentences, as they are ego centered.

Are words or phrases spoken that highlight a self-centered desire, as if his wife owes him? Too often married couples act in this self-serving fashion. Most all wedding ceremonies, state something like: *"I ___ take you _____ to be my lawful, wedded wife, promising before God with my friends as witnesses, that I will be to her a faithful, loving & devoted husband, that I will Honor her, LOVE her & remain with her in sickness & in health, in prosperity & in adversity & forsaking all others, and keep myself for her, & Her Only, as long as we both shall live?"*

Remember saying those words or something very similar at the altar? Go back through the words; they profess devotion to each other, and not what each partner **gets** from the another. Even when a couple makes their own vows, they each devoted themselves to each other in those promises before so many witnesses. The important point is to realize that they professed their life **to each other, not to themselves**.

Couples enter marriage looking for the ideal,

then they start living an ordeal,

and finally they get a new deal!

So, where did these unmet expectations come from? This is not a male versus female problem. Each side has a similar deficient ideal for marriage. They tend is to have self-gratifying expectations in their head and not express those unrealistic romantic outlooks to their prospective spouse before they get to the altar. Then, when she does not meet his desires, he becomes disenchanted with the relationship and eventually seeks a divorce. How do we ensure your marriage does not experience the unmet expectations as fifty percent of couples do each year?

> *True intimacy is this deep essence in a marriage, focused on the well being of their life mate.*
>
> *What God!"*

Remember the purpose here is to break down any walls of communication resistance that have formed and learn to effectively discuss each other's core desires. Look for ways to create a closer-knit union between you and your wife. To enhance intimate communication, someone has to go first, right? Keep in mind the purpose here is to **release the unmet expectations** between you and your wife. Relax and have some fun with it.

a. Make a quick list of the preliminary items you want to discuss together. Before the list is compiled, list a couple of her strengths. A proven technique for bringing up sensitive items is to jot down three or four desires on a piece of paper and exchange the notes at the same time to each other. Set a time when there are no distractions and the discussion can flow openly.

b. Be sure to affirm love out loud before any areas of discomfort or thoughts are brought up. Share the initial expectations for your marriage as though this is the first time she ever heard these words.

c. Try to frame the ideas being expressed in the first person. Use "I" and not "You." Perhaps state, "I believed that in our marriage I am . . . (list your first idea)" Then use a similar phrase to state your next thoughts from your perspective. When this format is used, she is not the "bad person." Simply state something to be included in the marriage. Be kind hearted and gentle towards her. Create an atmosphere where both parties experience a profound emotional connectedness to the entire marriage.

d. Encourage her through this exercise, as it will become a bridge for future open communications of deeper intimacy. Intimacy is not the same as sexual union. A couple is intimate in their sexual activities; however, they can become intimate in other ways as well.

Trust is a power that can be tenderly strengthened through these avenues of communication. Like a set of closed doors over the heart, both partners come to this exercise with an amount of fear of the unknown. At first, each individual "door" is only slightly opened. Bask in the genuine concern for each other, and your hearts will open their differing experiences for each other. This builds secure intimacy, which only a husband and wife were designed to experience. Be kind to one to another as you grow in trust within the marriage. Your relationship can be opened or shut based on the collective confidence in each other.

Secret # 3 – Defensiveness creates barriers not bridges: learn how to disarm these distrustful barriers

In the various martial arts, much time is spent learning how to defend yourself against an opponent. One who is highly skilled may never have a crushing blow penetrate his defenses. Men too often have this same mindset concerning their wives. A husband keeps her at arm's length so he is internally protected. The sad reality is that he pledged to allow this wonderful woman into every part of his life, yet instinctively he becomes defensive in too many areas. But wait just a minute! His wife is *not* his opponent; she is the most precious ingredient of his life. She is the only person allowed into his most private inner being.

Defensiveness is often followed quickly by pride, which stimulates his anger to swell up. Anger is then fanned when he does not feel his wife understands his viewpoint or has somehow violated him. Anger closes down his thoughtfulness for his wife. A wife can sense this emotional distance created by an angry wall, and then she begins to raise her own defenses. When the husband is not willing to yield his will, a barricade is built. Having a defensive posture, verbally or in some other form, shuts his wife out.

How can a husband keep from erecting these
emotional barriers?
How do the barriers get torn down?

First, let's address "How does a husband keep from forming walls of separation in the first place?" A quick solution, which once it becomes a habit can be virtually bulletproof, is to create a neutral signal that both partners recognize. The "time-out" signal is fast and easy to use. A referee or a player in a game places his one hand into the palm of the other hand forming a "T." This signals the referee or the sidelines that they want a "time-out." This same hand gesture will work effectively with a wife as well. When the husband feels his blood pressure rising or he can't understand what she is saying, he can ask for a "timeout" to gain clarification.

This hand motion signals to her that he needs greater clarification. Sometimes, what the wife says sends a mixed signal to her husband from some earlier discussion or situation. So, he seeks clarification of the details. Remember that when a person fully comprehends his wife's desires, he can rationally process the information. If she "hits him" with some off-the-wall issue or description, he might tend to build a wall of resentment. Whenever he senses a disconnect at the base level of her conversation, he can ask for a timeout to get clarification.

This problem is magnified when he is trying to perceive her information and she becomes more intense by the minute. Now, what does he do once he sees the walls of isolation are rising?

A quick "time out" might still be in order but, this time, for a brief break from the action. Calmly and in a low voice, tell her to give you a couple minutes to more fully process what she is saying. When the discussion resumes, perhaps say something like, "Ok, this is what I hear you saying . . ." or, "Is that what you want me to hear?" Or say, "Are you wanting me to try to figure out . . .?" or "Do you just want to let off some steam . . .?" Seek to clarify the issues and let her know that you are listening with both mind and heart. It is important for wives to have their husband's heart in tune with theirs. Since we approach issues from a different vantage point, one partner might be searching for an answer in the wrong direction. Clarification can build emotional intimacy where pride tears apart expressive closeness.

A very practical application of this "digestive method" is that we sometimes present an idea to each other with the object of letting the idea "brew" a bit before the discussion takes place. Couples can develop a code for this course of action to prepare the other person for the discussion to take place later on. Either spouse can bring a new thought for consideration to the other partner by telling the other something like, "Hey, I need to speak to you about an issue that will take a bit to explain. Can you give me a few minutes to share an idea to work on for me?" The other person might say "OK, what is it about?" and the first one explains in a few brief sentences what the subject is or gives a couple of details, and then both know the topic is high on the agenda when they can focus on the specific item being brought up.

Another technique when a problem is already a bit heated is to take a couple of minutes and write down what each person is hearing from the other. Keep the notes brief. It is important for each side to be heard. It is equally important for each side to hear the other person. As the Bible shows in James 1:19, "be quick to hear, slow to speak and slow to anger." Boy, I wish I did that all the time! However, when practiced, it works extremely well.

Perhaps a problem starts out as an innocent statement which gets taken out of context or not fully seen the way it was first expressed. The tendency is to go on the offensive. Attack! But wait there is another way to solve this heated argument..

Secret # 4 – Attack the problem and not each other.

Verbally attacking a person will establish more walls or barriers as we discussed in # 3 from the other perspective. In # 3 we saw that defensiveness makes that person erect their own barriers. Here we see that attacking your spouse causes the other person to form those barriers or withdraw to form defensive positions. In either case, effective communication is restricted whenever a barrier is built. These walls can be constructed extremely fast. Sometimes it seems we carry around mental blockages to guard yourself from everyone. In a marriage, walls need to be destroyed and intimacy becomes the norm. A close relationship is framed from letting the other person into our heart and not from creating barriers which isolate yourself.

Your initial tactic is to recognize what the problem is that has you both steamed up. Being verbally aggressive to one another is a sure fire way to create more heat instead of understanding. So take a moment to see what got you to this point to determine why you are at such odds with each other?

Ask questions similar to these:

> 1 – Does she really know what point I am trying to express? You might gently stop her for a few seconds and ask her to re-frame her position in her own words. Perhaps tell her that you want to be sure you have the right picture for her thoughts.

> 2 – Am I missing something she said about this idea? You might say, "OK so what I hear you saying is …"

> 3 – Am I just trying to win an argument or trying to get her heart's desires about this?

4 – Take a few seconds with the time out signal and ask her, "Would you put **your side** of the problem in a few different words please."

5 – What is my ultimate reason for pushing the issue here? Are our relationship and my love for her at the core of my words?

These are reflective thoughts to let digest within your mind to get you focused on your wife. They also help you to not force a selfish issue at her.

Don't play the blame game. Blaming each other is another form of a personal verbal attack. To ensure that your ego is set aside think about your accusations before you spit them out at your spouse. Sometimes the way an idea is presented comes across imposes the accusation upon them when they may have not been guilty of the actions as you perceive them.

Use the word "I" and not "you" in stating your issues or when asking your questions. "You" comes across as being critical of your wife even if that is not your desire. "I" shows you are taking personal possession for your thoughts. It tends to soften the edges when a person takes ownership for their ideas.

Too often, we might retain deep-seated problems that erode the delicate balance for a marriage. What if the problem-solving has not worked for us thus far, where you are in the middle of a heated verbal exchange and one person has exited in a hurt or hurtful manner? What should you do next? How can the problem be fixed?

Secret # 5 will add to the process.

Secret # 5 – True communication involves repeated forgiveness from both life partners.

Sincere communication will begin with honest forgiveness. This is not an easy solution to the problem because feelings are hurt and cutting words have been hurled at one another, thus establishing the need for forgiveness. One person has to make the first move. Of course it is more palatable if one spouse is on their way to apologize to the other and they bump into each other coming to make up. That does not happen every time, right? So let's examine forgiveness and its true message of healing for married couples. Keep repeating within your mind, **"Forgiveness is a gift I give myself."**

When we speak about forgiveness, remember that only one entity can actually "forgive and forget," and He is God. People do not forget since they do not have the ability to completely erase a situation from their brain. We may try to bury the issues or the attached emotions such as anger, but we relive the entire irritating episode immediately when something appropriate triggers that memory. The trigger can be from out of nowhere by someone mentioning something that they did not realize was an instant reminder for you. It can be a certain song or a particular fragrance, or it might be a word or an expression. It can be as harmless as someone's particular voice. You do not have to always concentrate on a certain event for that event, with all its emotional baggage, to come flooding into your experience.

As soon as I began to write the issues in Chapters One and Two, about my mom and dad arguing out in front of our house in Florida at age thirteen, I was instantly there again. I saw the car, the street, the other houses, and of course I heard the words violently shouted by mom and dad from fifty years ago. It is impossible for me to erase those memories. However, I did wash over the event with a large amount of forgiveness for both persons, so I do not feel the attached sting that troubled me for so many years, nor do I suffer from the pain attached to those "mind movies" that play inside my head. They are somehow detached from my heart and a distant, yet still distinct, memory. However, the memory is vivid and non-erasable. I cannot forget that event. So it is with many occurrences from marriage that we lived through.

It seems that when we have some sharp emotional attachment, whether cherished or disappointing thoughts, those mental movies are easily replayed for viewing. I do not call up every specific event that has happened between Elaine and me over our many years together. Yet I can mention a particular significant time between us to Elaine, and we at both transported to that time and place. We each have our own special thoughts, but those memories burn brightly. Whenever I think about or hear the song "Time in a bottle" by Jim Croce, I instantly "see" Elaine starting down the aisle in the back of the church building, and I get a lump in my throat. She is still my bride! The pleasant memory is alive.

My point is that people cannot "forget" as much as they would like to put out of their mind. Sometimes a person wants to erase some various memories in their marriage. If they had a fight where they said unkind and damaging words to each other, the movie is ready. If they had great "make-up sex" following the anger and verbal jousts hurled at each other, those memories are also there.

Do not feel less of a person because a memory in particular details which happened years ago is still present. Learn to forgive a life partner as it is the most therapeutic salve you can apply to any intimacy. Practice forgiveness often and generously. It does not harm a person's character or marriage; it enhances it. Remember that forgiveness is a gift you give yourself. Forgiveness frees a person from so many negative maladies that plague couples.

What if every husband and wife learned to practice honest forgiveness toward each other? How would this revolutionize each relationship? How does one express or receive forgiveness? Can he squash pride to let his life partner know who much he truly loves her? How well does he accept forgiveness? Wash over the negative pain with the cleansing power of gentle mercy. Do not use hurt feelings as a club or wedge and say, "Ah ha, I knew you couldn't let that go!" when the wife might repeat a problem she said she would "never" do again. How many times must a husband forgive his wife? As often as she violates him and needs forgiveness.

Receiving forgiveness might be more difficult than extending mercy to the other person. The very need for forgiveness shows that emotional hurt has transpired. Receiving a kindness such as unconditional mercy might come with "baggage," such as certain conditions or a hidden agenda. When the person who created the trouble tries to patch up the situation, it is natural to wonder when they will explode again? Take the high road and, whenever she offers that she is sorry for the wrongs inflicted, literally embrace her to show forgiveness to her. Typically a hug is greatly appreciated. As often as she is wrong, forgive her.

Perhaps the husband is the one who needs the mercy extended to him, and he is trying to relay his heartfelt desire to make it right again and his wife is not so willing to be generous. Does he feel he is being made to "jump through some hoops" to show his sincerity? Keep trying to do all that is possible to patch it back the way it was before the blowup. Keep in mind that the wife is a person with her share of internal issues. At times, she may have a harder time accepting his peace offering. Be sincere and consistent in the apologies and be patient with her response. True love seeks the best in the other person. Keep seeking to help each other grow in the marriage.

In either direction, this process can last a while and the "offended" one can make the other party squirm a bit. If the husband sets his sights on submitting to his wife, he will be at peace for working towards the resolution. Keep the issues that caused the separation at a distance in your mind. If it was some small incident that grew out of proportion, do not bring it up again. If it was a legitimate problem that needs to be addressed, take the time and be gentle in the presentation of the issue again, lest it create the negative explosion all over again.

Perhaps as mentioned above, write out your understanding no matter which *side* of the issue you find yourself. Write down or type up both sides of the present bad discussion. Write out her side also, as best you understand it to be. Often when a problem is reduced to writing, it gives both parties the opportunity to view more easily. Then lovingly, ask her if this is what she was saying and what she meant to share when the problem erupted. Ask her what her impressions are of both sides for the issue.

Express your love to her all along the way. Learn to listen to the intent behind the words. In this way, she will see that you are listening to her heart as well as her words. Develop finely tuned listening skills, as these will serve you well for many years to come.

Secret #6 – Develop discerning listening skills.

Do you hear what I hear? Women have a highly developed sensitive side. It is easy for a husband to crush his wife's ideas if he is not careful. The entire next chapter (Chapter 5) is entirely devoted to a husband's diligent listening, so we will not spend time here discussing it. Active listening for a husband is a delicate mixture of emotion, intelligence, and a heavy dose of tact.

We do feel that these six suggestions can disarm most arguments if some forethought is applied.

Since this chapter is to aide in intimate interactive communication, these PEP PILLS will further assist you in drawing closer as a couple.

"PEP PILLS" for your marriage –
Communication Action Steps For A Better Marital Relationship

HAVE FUN WITH THESE *"PEP PILLS"*

Remember that your relationship is more important than any single problem which exists between you two.

 # 1 – Play this game – "Remember When?" Start an open communication game of "Remember When?" by asking her what are some of her fondest memories from your marriage so far? **Hint:** be prepared with a brief list of notes about some of the highlights you remember. If needed, joke with her that you need a few "cheat sheet notes."

If she needs some help "remembering," start her off with "Do you remember when we went . . ." (and include an upbeat feeling you experienced on a certain fun trip or date you fondly keep in mind). Ask her what she also remembered about that certain event. (Don't get angry if she does not call to mind precisely what you did about that day or trip.)

Whenever she starts to really open up, let her go and enjoy her mind movies right along with her. Encourage her to include any details and politely ask what she enjoyed from that experience. Don't try to read her mind. If there is something you can't quite sort out, ask her about those specific details. "I'm trying to figure out, which restaurant did we go to?" or some other "hook" that connects the memory for both of you.

This exercise is to build your positive life movie experiences for more creative understanding between you two. Familiarity breeds intensity for a married couple. Intense personal communication develops a profound warm relationship.

Take this *PEP PILL* #1 often down memory lane to enhance your wonderful loving experiences. Plan a specific date-night topic, where you reminisce through dates you shared during or even before marriage.

 # 2 – After # 1 has been done a few separate times, ask her some deeper more sensitive questions, such as:

"Is there something I have done that causes you to trust me less or to not have as much faith in me as you once had?"

"What do you need from me so that you can feel more cherished?"

"What can I do to make you feel more secure?"

"Are there any needs you have which are not being met now?"

"Is there something you want me to help you develop in yourself?"

Consider that she might turn this around and ask you similar questions, so be prepared to give some open and honest answers. If respect is high on your list of personal needs, have a couple of questions related to how your wife might develop this area for you. For instance:

"What are four ways you respect my leadership?"

"How well do you feel I do . . ." (place at the end of the question something she needs to recognize more about you.)

"What positive habits would you like to see me develop a bit more?"

This process is to develop the relationship to a much deeper level. These rewards can run in a profound direction from the work put into this segment of the relationship. The more that is invested into these PEP PILLS, the more the marriage will flourish.

Always expect the best for your marriage!

CHAPTER 5

Do You Hear What I Hear?
Heartfelt listening to your spouse:

This Chapter is About Active Listening Skills for Husbands who Want to Truly Pay Attention to Their Wives. Learning to Understand How a Wife Talks so You Can Hear What her Heart Says.

It is annoying when a husband expresses ideas that land on "deaf ears." Or he tells his wife there is something important to speak about and after the problem is laid out, and she says something like, "OK, I see" and then nods her head and leaves without giving any actual feedback? Or perhaps there is some distressing situation to share with her, and she seems completely disconnected? Issues arise everyday in a relationship that could become inflamed. Through this chapter, these situations and several problematic issues in a marriage will be discussed with some solutions presented as well.

When a husband pays attention to his wife, he sends a strong message to her that declares, "you are important to me." Active listening shows concern about her thoughts and feelings, which is important to her. Listening without becoming defensive encourages open and honest sharing. When a husband can practice effective communication, he will strengthen their close relationship and create a strong marital foundation.

Women often have a highly developed sensitive side called their emotions. It is easy for a husband to crush his wife's ideas if he is not careful. This chapter is about enhancing the listening skills of the husband in numerous areas. This listening-skills development focuses on enriching the marriage communication experience. It is essential to pay attention to her struggles, as this is the only way to get at the root causes of any concern. It is easy for guys to accidently squash their wife's thoughts if they are not careful. A wise husband will take the time to share open dialog with his wife.

Artful Listening for a Husband is a Delicate Mixture of Emotion and Intellect, Combined with a Measure of Intentional Tact

Listening is certainly a part of communication. However, for men, listening is different than how their wife "*listens.*" Notice the emphasis is on the **cycle or the sequence of information exchanged,** rather than just a couple simply swapping a few ideas back and forth. Effective communication involves receiving information, then allowing time to assimilate this data so the second person can wisely respond. The more important the ideas, the longer it may take to fully complete the cycle for this information process. It may feel a bit awkward to change listening habits at first, but a marriage is well worth that time investment.

People process new information differently. One person can digest an entire new vision quickly, while a second partner takes days to let the thought rattle around. Neither method is incorrect; some people just digest information at a different rate. My wife generally does not answer as quickly as I do in our discussions. This does not mean she is not interested or that she has no ideas to formulate about the subject. She processes information in a different fashion from the way I process ideas. At first in our marriage, this lag time between a new idea brought up and her eventual response seemed to indicate a lack of respect towards me. That is not the case. Elaine is very smart and incredibly wise. However, we process new information in our own particular fashion. In general, men and women process concepts and information uniquely different from one another. Do you know how your wife actually records new thoughts in her brain? If you are not careful, you may conclude that her unique mode of knowledge digestion is inadequate, when truthfully she is simply unlike you in this area.

How Do Men and Women Process and Communicate Information?

To compound the issues a bit more, not only do the genders process information in different methods within the mind, we each have diverse needs when it comes to expressing our own ideas. Women often need to articulate their issues to rehearse the unique circumstances to someone else without receiving specific advice or answers from that other person. This is a difficult discipline for most men to accept as they usually digest information and solve problems, unlike most females. Women seem to voice their problems and arrange the answers they need as the conversation goes along. Women often have an inert need to express more details than most men. This does not make either gender wrong; it merely reveals our distinctiveness. Typically women are not seeking solutions to their problems at the moment and in the same manner as men do since basically they just want to express their issues. If a wife wants some solutions to her dilemma, she might ask for help with a particular situation. However, if she does not ask for specific advice but still wants to discuss a specific concern, then accept this as her usual problem-solution process, to vent, which is counter to how men typically work through problematic issues. Wives do not often want their husband to supply insights for her problems at this point. Here is a personal insight over this issue of male versus female problem solving. Keep in mind that, as men, we usually need to generate solutions when a problem is presented.

Allow this incident to clarify the gender misunderstandings often encountered by husbands and wives. One time, Elaine was having some very trying times at work. After suffering through the mess at work, she often came home distraught and upset at the situation. She is an optimistic and humble woman who does not become easily discouraged, so it was apparent that work was awfully upsetting to her. It was obvious that she needed help. So, we sat and discussed the issues she faced each day. Unfortunately, how I responded was not what she needed. She would come home, and I would listen intently to her impassioned cry for help, or so I thought it was a cry for help. After a while of patient listening, I had compiled a great set of solutions for her, which I related as gently as possible. I am really good at fixing things! The next few days, I waited to see if my suggestions were useful. However, when she verbally went off again, I pondered as to why my ideas did not work? I asked her which solutions I gave her did not help so we could work out a few better alternatives? She looked at me as if I was painted green! She said, "I don't need you to fix the situation, I just need for you to listen to me!" With that, she got up, and I was dumbfounded at her comments. I felt bewildered since I could not help my wife at a time she really needed me. I felt like I was a failure!

Actually the true answer surfaced some time later from a book I read about marriage relationships. While reading how men and women process thoughts or problems, the author mentioned that wives do not want to express their issues to their husband so he will become the "knight in shining armor" and rescue her. (I was shocked!) He went on to say that a wife wants to "declare" her problems and have him actively listen to the words that are coming straight from her heart. I admit, I did not help Elaine the way she needed me to help her through this set of work-related problems. Women reading this book know where I went wrong.

I tried to listen as a man listens. Therefore, I attempted to solve her problems, which she did not actually want to have solved in the manner presented. Women do not need to have their problems "resolved" by their husband. Most often they simply want to be heard. A wife might say to her husband something like, "I need to talk to you." He determines that she is having a bad day, which does not necessarily mean what he thinks it means. Keep in mind that men and women do problem-solving differently. This will get addressed in a bit.

Men Become Distraught by Their Wives as well, for the Opposite Reason

The opposite communication disaster is true from wives to their husband when it comes to handling his problems. It is often wearisome for him, when his wife listens as a woman, since her husband is describing an important problem he is having which he needs her help to resolve. The reason it is distressing for this man is that his wife concentrates on the situation as she might listen with one of her friends. Often, men look for their wife to supply some solutions to their dilemmas. When she listens but does not generate any constructive feedback, he thinks she does not care!

Early in our marriage, I mistook my wife's hesitancy and non-verbal response for a lack of interest. I would tell Elaine about an issue that had me baffled which got no apparent thoughts through to her. She would hear my words or questions and simply walk away as though I was not even in the same room. She said nothing and did not even nod; she just left! I was insulted and became angry since she did not make any comments at all. She did not understand that I needed a slight indication that she heard me. She could at least have indicated that she would get back to me with some consideration of the issue at hand. Women do not realize the gravity of this lack of action on a man's self image. Men take it as a huge show of disrespect.

Imagine that! She acts like a woman, and we act like a man, and neither one is sure why the other person does not "get it" or is upset over this inactivity.

This is one chapter to be highlighted by both partners and to discuss how they want to be listened to by the other person. Let's notice some solutions for effectively "hearing" one another so each spouse has their individual needs met.

For husbands, here is an easy way to determine **how** your wife wants to be heard. As she introduces a problem or sensitive issue, bring in the time-tested hand signal for a "time-out." In a game, the player or coach is letting the referee know he needs to take a brief break.

A husband can do this for his wife to more clearly determine what she wants: listening or fixing. He will gain greater clarification to which direction she wants him to proceed. It can become an easy ritual whenever he begins to place his hands together; his wife will let him know his role is in this current conversation. This can tremendously help to show what her expectations are at this time.

Wives, Your Husband Wants to *LISTE*N, as You Need Him to Listen – To You

For wives, please understand that husbands want to give their wife what she is seeking in this area of intimate communication. Since men and women have different communication needs, help him know how to accurately listen. He is trying to figure out what his next step is to help her. Discuss this together to develop greater clarity for future communications. Either use the "timeout" signal or express up front how he should actively listen in any particular conversation.

Ladies, husbands need their wives to listen to them unlike how two women listen to each other. He does not need for his wife to hear the words, nod once or twice, and then when he is done, she just leaves the discussion. While this is how women communicate with their female friends, just remember, husbands are men! I felt insulted when I was treated this way! *Without realizing it, a wife is treating her husband with complete disrespect by offering him no solutions for the issues he has raised.*

Try this type of listening

Because we process information differently, here is what spouses can do for each other. When a husband wants his wife to generate some solutions to a particular predicament, he can give her the important details to the problem and let it "cook" with her for a while. She will listen and then express to him that she needs time to think it through. When they get back together to discuss it further, she has had the time to think about the dilemma. This way, if she wants to, she can let it rumble around in her mind for a while before making any constructive comments. Sometimes she has a few extra questions to assess the situation, and if needed, she will come back for clarification while working on the issue. Then they can get together to talk about the difficulty presented. It might happen that she will have some insights for consideration or she will let him know that she cannot come up with any solutions at all. There might be problems presented where the wife worked on those issues and was unable to generate any additional suggestions. That is an acceptable solution as her husband knows she heard his situation and then worked on it a while. In this way, both partners received what they needed to process the information for each other.

For some couples, this illustration mentioned above is reversed, and it is the husband who needs the time to reflect on the ideas before he comments, whereas his wife is quick to discern a resolution. Within each marriage, the one who needs the space to process an item and which spouse comes up with answers quickly is different. Be patient and considerate of one another, as men and women differ from each other since God "wired" them that way. Enjoy the diversity!

Men and Women Process Information in Their own Way

After speaking with many wives in our seminars, it became clear that they did not mean to be disrespectful to their husband, and they did not understand why a man would feel insulted by their actions. Ladies, please acknowledge that something was presented and that you will think about it and get back to him. Many husbands feel acknowledged and appreciated by a quick verbal gesture from their wife. Husbands expressed a feeling of being ignored, and their wife was shocked that he felt this way since she acted as a normal woman would act. The wife did not try to convey to her husband an uncaring attitude. This is certainly another way that communication is perceived and delivered, separate from the intended purpose. Husbands, initiate this cleansing dialog today so the marriage becomes stronger through interactive communication.

Verbal Communication for a Husband and a Wife is a Circular Arrangement of Information Interchange

The basic idea of communication involves receiving data or information, letting it "penetrate" into the mind, and then responding back to the other person in the discussion. This actual cycle may only take a few seconds or it may require several days for idea's absorption and contemplation.

How Does a Husband Tenderly Let his Wife Know her Actions are Bothering Him?

❖ Start with the end in mind. What outcome is desired in this sensitive discussion? How should she consider his feelings about respect? What does the actual conversation progress and what is the desired result? Don't let negative feedback from previous similar circumstances warp this healthy communication progress. Focus on how the "perfect" dialog would go, and mentally rehearse that conversation several times.

❖ To create the most positive situation, list out seven or eight of her best assets before the conversation. This is a list of personal qualities and not her physical attributes. Go ahead and put them on a piece of paper. Keep them close at hand during the discussion to avoid a possible negative tone. It will help to refocus on her greatest assets!

❖ If time alone is difficult to arrange, let her know there is something important to be discussed. Mention some of the ideas for the discussion in summary form, so she can better process what is to be discussed.

❖ When the time is set for the conversation, think through the specific prepared questions and statements. If necessary, write out each question or statement that is to be presented. Look at them and imagine how to pose them to her. Leave the actual process for the conversation a bit loose. Create a general flow for the information to be covered.

❖ One way to open the conversation is to circle a particular paragraph in a book that states the specific thoughts to address. Perhaps highlight something in this book to cover with her. Show these circled paragraphs to her, asking what she feels about the ideas being presented. Give her time to digest the information, and even ask some clarifying questions. This practice has been a great way for other husbands to open up non-confrontational conversations with their wives when they did not understand the woman's viewpoint.

❖ Be sure to gently open up her heart. Seek to create pleasant dialog.

❖ Maintain eye contact as the questions are asked. Looking into her eyes is fitting for open dialog to occur. She wants to look deep into your soul as the dialog flows along. Enjoy this time of mutual verbal intimacy.

How Can Active Listening Quickly Break Down?

Why do general conversations stop working and how can a couple get those damaged conversations back on track? Here are seven examples of reasons why the communication process might fall apart and some possible strategies for dealing with these communication difficulties.

1. Sometimes a husband makes the assumption that he "already knows" what she is going to say. Any husband married for a while feels he can read his wife's mind. **Be cautious here!** Just because one can finish a person's sentences sometimes, does not give him the right to assume he knows what she wants to say. Many husbands have attempted to finish their wife's sentence only to hear her say, "No that's not at all what I was going to say!" Knowing a great deal about someone is terrific. However, a husband who believes he knows what his wife would **always** say before she says it, is on dangerous footing and is often perceived as rude.

To eliminate this habit, be sure to let her finish her entire thought first. After this, if he has an additional thought, he could ask her something such as, "OK, I see what you mean, would this also fit in with that idea?" Then he can state what he was going to suggest in the first place after having heard her full thought process. Keep in mind that she may have something entirely different to say.

2. The listening process can break down when a husband receives a different message than what he was expecting. Perhaps he thinks that an idea was crystal clear in his mind only to find out that how he initially interpreted it was not in line with her thinking at all. All of a sudden he is in "*deep water*" when her idea is clearly verbalized. Perhaps he was looking for her to validate his beliefs or assumptions, and she goes off in a different direction from what he expected of her. When this happens, his listening skills shut down and tune her out. He might respond out loud with irritation in his voice, "What did you just say?" If expressed a bit louder than she is expecting, she may also start to shut down her active listening. Now two people are emotionally heading in the opposite direction about a concept neither intended to pursue in the first place.

    To help defuse this problem, each person can take a moment to reflect on the incident and say something like, "I think we are on different wave lengths here." Acknowledge that what was said was obviously not what she heard and that you need to go back through the discussion to be sure that both persons are on the same track. Be sure to "re-state" the important concepts using different words.

    It is very easy it is to make the wrong assumptions innocently. An incident that took place recently illustrates how an innocent mistake can wreck a discussion. After the fact, we chuckled about this two-day-long discussion, which unintentionally got extremely off target.

A situation can get out of sync quickly and you and your wife can be in a heated argument over some misdirected information which is not the fault of either one of you. . Let me give you a short true life example. Work through this example and see if you don't get caught up in the same fashion with your wife.

Here's what happened. I needed an address for a friend named Terry to whom I was writing a note of encouragement. I knew precisely who I need the address for. I asked my wife if she had Terry's address. Elaine said she might need to ask another friend of ours for the address who knew my buddy. When I looked at my wife with a puzzled expression on my face, she asked for more details. I did not understand why this particular third party came into the conversation, but I did not make too much of it and went about my business. On the following day, I approached my wife about the needed address. After a few more curious questions from her about such a simple address, I realized a possible disconnect between my request and her receiving of that question. It dawned on me that two days earlier we had discussed another person named Terry who lives in a different state. So, when I asked for "Terry's address," my wife thought I meant the friend who lives in Tennessee, and I was actually asking about the "Terry" who lives in our Pennsylvania. I knew who I was referring to all along but because my question was a bit obscure my wife misunderstood what I was seeking. Neither of us was "wrong" and it could have digressed into a big argument if we were not on guard for each other's feelings.

It may sound more long-winded in writing than how it played out, but it took a while to sort it all out. Yes, the note was sent to the right friend. In hindsight, it was my shortfall because if I had mentioned "Terry's" last name in the first place, it would have eliminated the confusion. So this was my fault for not making my request as clear as it could have been made. This incident had an easy fix to it and no real harm was done. But how often does a miscommunication get drawn out into a heated argument when both parties hear a uniquely divided message because of preconceived thoughts?

The instant a person senses that you are on two detached wavelengths, stop, and get clarification of the facts as they are perceived at that moment, and then start the conversation again. This sounds like it would take a while, but in reality, it only takes a few seconds to straighten out the confusion and communicate the intended ideas in the first place.

3. Active listening breaks down when two people get sidetracked by various additional commotions. It is difficult to have a serious discussion when there are frequent distractions going on. At home, it could be the kids, the TV, a computer game, or a cell phone.

When a serious discussion is necessary, get rid of all the distractions possible. Turn off the electronic devices, or at least put the phone on vibrate. Do not answer it unless a true emergency is pending.

A caution here for the husband: your wife might want to talk about something *SHE THINKS* is important, and after a few minutes, there is an urge to say, "I thought you wanted to talk about something important?" Don't be impolite; it might be significant to her. Let her share what she wants to express. Sometimes, she may simply want uninterrupted time with her husband. If this is an often-asked-for situation, schedule specific time each week to be with her, as she is shouting that she needs "alone time." Remember your dating days? You wanted to be alone with her and her only, right? Well the situation is reversed a bit, and she needs her husband to be fully invested in her information. If needed, take her to a local café for a cup of coffee or tea and spend time alone from all distractions. Let this be "your time."

6. For a husband, paying strict attention to his wife can regress if he becomes impatient and wants her to "get to the point"? Perhaps, it's been a tough day, and she wants to tell every detail of her day when you first walk through the door. Why does she have to go on and on over every tiny incident that happened to her through routine situations of her day? Can't a husband just have a few minutes to "chill out" a bit first instead of being bombarded by all this trivial information?

Keep in mind that men and women communicate differently. Women need to share these details as a way to bond and relieve stress. If you don't want this, gently ask for some form of acceptable guidelines for arrival at home to decompress for a specific short amount of time (we'll discuss this a bit more in the next chapter).

Perhaps the wife also works and wants to tell everything that happened to her. Relieve some of her load by caring for the kids? How about getting the supper started? Does the table need to be set before sitting down to relax? In our frenzied lifestyle these days, many wives work outside the house, and so they are tired and need "down time" as well. Seek to generate whatever she needs to relax and look forward to being home.

7. Too often husbands listen only enough to "reload" so they can be equipped for the next verbal volley. Men tend to be competitive, so they try to "win" the discussion even if it is not an argument. They tend to feel the urge to be ready with a counter attack or to have the right defense set to block any incoming assaults. If the situation gets

heated, it is very easy to become extra defensive instead of focusing on her thoughts.

How can we avoid creating a defensive posture when the wife is presenting information? First, simply listen to the information and how she is presenting it. If the situation is testy and an argument is rising, really listen and tone down your words. "A soft answer turns away wrath" (Proverbs 15:1) James said, "Know this, my beloved brothers: let every person be quick to hear, slow to speak, slow to anger; for the anger of man does not produce the righteousness of God." (James 1:19–20) We have two ears and one mouth for an important reminder. I am the first to say that it takes two people to argue. If one will not be drawn in to the fray, an argument will not develop.

You will find that the second "PEP PILL" at the end of this chapter is a three-minute session for your wife to share any information she wants. Following her verbal presentation, the same amount of time will be arranged, to repeat back to her what she has just said. In my marriage seminars, most wives express that this is the first time their husbands have ever totally focused on their words. The husbands say that they are a bit nervous since they have not had to repeat back to their wife so precisely what she is saying. Initiating this exercise may thrill the wife and generate extra husband points in her eyes.

8. Avoid the vague generalities, since it is irritating for one person to say, "hey, we need to talk," and then give no details at all about the subject matter. This does not allow the second partner to visualize how important the subject is under consideration. Imagine if an issue or project needed to be presented a boss at work (or if you are the boss, think of how it might look if a worker acted this way). Would you just drop some verbal surprise on your boss as they passed the office or sent some nebulous

email saying, "we've got a situation"? If you are courteous about their time, you will qualify the issue for your boss ahead so they can set aside the appropriate amount of time to handle the situation. So, how do you treat your wife?

Is a wife to be treated with less courtesy than you would someone at work? Stories abound that husbands or wives treats their co-workers with more dignity than they do their spouses. What's up with that? Wives deserve the very best their husband has to offer. One particular important time of the day is when they greet each other at home after work. Too often the conversation, based on how either partner's day went, does not show tenderness towards each other. This can set a negative tone for the whole evening. What if, instead, they chose to radically change the evening format with a specific effort to always make the day great at home?

Before going to the next part of the chapter, think about your arrivals home over the last couple of months. Were your work issues still with you? Was she treated as though she was somehow responsible for what happened all day? Is she expected to be in a great mood no matter what she was forced to handle during her day? Why not be the positive pace setter for the evening? I am not suggesting you do cartwheels or act like a clown. Simply, become the head of the house in all areas of the marriage, even the emotional mood, and especially upon initially arriving at home.

So Husbands, Be Sure to Actively Listen

❖ Be eagerly present. Discover what her day was like. Ask her, not simply "how was your day?" but dig a bit deeper in the discussion, "What were three (or some desired number) specific things that happened today?" If you remember some of the events she mentioned about her day such as shopping, visiting with a particular friend or going some definite place you can ask her about those. For instance if she was going shopping did she find the dress she needed? How was your visit with "Joan".   The purpose for this exchange is to show how much she is cared for. Let her show by her response that she enjoys the added interest in her. Be in the moment when she shares the details from her day.

You can set this afternoon discussion early on by asking what she has planned for her day. Make some mental notes to reflect back to her in the evening.

❖ To further set the mood, have her beverage of choice waiting when she comes home. If she gets home first, and she does not have anything to drink, go get it for her. Be observant and responsive to her. Then sit down close to her and ask some of these questions listed in this section or some others that would be thoughtful.

❖ Be present in her conversations. Try to focus on what she is sharing. Be a bit verbal by stating small points back to her such as: "I see," "hmmm, that's interesting." And be sure to reword it back to her, but be careful not to break up her conversation or train of thought too much.

❖ Listen to the whole thought. If she is going on to another subject, be sure you clarify the change in direction. Show interest; certainly do not act uninterested in the change of direction.

❖ Control your emotions. Keep in mind that two people typically do not see every situation in the same fashion. If your wife's message is causing a strong response, acknowledge these emotions to her. Try to keep them from interfering with the focus on her situation.

❖ Look at the situation through her eyes. Work to understand her perspective in the matter under discussion. Empathy means to look at her message with kindness. Try to listen with emotions in check as mentioned in the last point. Work to seek what she is driving at rather than jumping to a rapid conclusion, as if it is all figured out quickly.

Husband – Active listening requires a response, but not necessarily an opinion

Keep in mind this chapter is about active listening skills for husbands who want to pay closer attention to their wives.

PEP PILLS for Active Listening in Your Marriage: Action Steps for a Better Marriage Relationship

 # 1 – Open-ended sentences – ask a series of specific questions, and just listen to her. Let her know your desire to find out more about her. She can speak about anything she wants to share. Ask questions related to her dreams that she has shared before. This communicates to her a desire to hear what she has to say. Learn to focus on her needs. Listen to what she wants in life. Zone in on her deep-seated needs. Keep in mind, this book is written for a husband to focus on his wife.

Questions could be something like this:

Honey, how would you finish this sentence? "Someday I would really like to . . ."

"A special vacation you would like to take would be . . ."

"If time and money were no object, what would you really like to do?"

(If you need any other suggestions, just email me, and I will be glad to oblige!)

At first, she might be looking for the hidden agenda, so encourage her that this is no hoax; having her share her needs is paramount. Ask some open-ended questions to get the discussion started, especially if genuine verbal communication has not been vibrant in the marriage.

#2 – The 3-minute timer – This is a special experience she is going to enjoy. You will listen to her in an undivided fashion for 3 minutes, where she can share anything she wants to. It can be about her day, her friends, or whatever she wants to share. This is to become a better listener for her. You will set a timer, and at the end of the 3 minutes, tell her what she spoke about. Hint, just soak it up and don't try to "memorize" her words. Reflect back to her as much as possible. Make sure she understands that the words reflected back might be phrased a bit differently than her words. So, if she generates a huge amount of details, squish those details down a bit, and encourage her to appreciate the verbal differences between men and women. Be patient with her. Try to share in your response as many details as possible, especially if she is detail oriented.

Ask her if she enjoyed doing this together? If she responds in some form of "yes!" then ask her how often she would like to do it again? The point is to meet her emotional needs in this exercise. Always focus on your wife! This practice will pay great dividends. :)

#3 – Remain available for her to express herself – Ask her how her day went then without any interruptions; let her spill the details as she desires. Simply listen attentively without forming any rebuttals for problems she might bring up. Nod or make very brief comments that concern the details, nothing more.

Your wife needs your attention, not necessarily your advice.

#4 - As you stimulate conversations stay with her emotions and look at the situation through her eyes. Work to understand her perspective in the matter under discussion. You can ask clarifying questions such as

"Could you go back over that for me." or "OK so I missed a point here so help me out, just what did you mean by (then restate what part you understand before getting a bit sidetracked)" Avoid jumping to rapid   conclusions as if it is all figured out quickly. The purpose here is to let her share any information she desires.

#5 - Since women use conversation as an emotional connection device and men use conversation as a learning experience this Pep Pill will help you learn and your wife connect to you closer - Ask a couple of these questions to bond more with her.

Help me learn about your desires, give me three specific ways I can help you around the house.

Why do you think your friendship with (insert her best friend's name) is so tight?

How do you feel I am a good husband? ("father" also works well here)

Listen to how she expresses these ideas and incorporate some additional beliefs that are similar. She is   sharing what are some of her values.

This is a general ongoing project to do:
To become the best husband possible, practice "watching" how women converse with each other. Listen to their conversations. Take note that they do not exchange information in the same structure as men, nor are they looking for the same responses as men desire with other men in your conversations. Applying these subtle differences in how women transfer data can alter a marriage big time. An effective husband continually develops his acute listening skills. Your wife will appreciate that you can tune into her heart through her discussions.

Always expect the best for your marriage!

CHAPTER 6

Defuse the time bomb before it blows! Learn how to manage stressful situations that occur in marriage.

How do husbands and wives help each other relieve the pressure life throws at them? Stress is an everyday occurrence. Numerous times throughout the day, emotional pressures creep in, no matter how much a person tries to avoid this tension. So, how well do people personally cope with the issues they encounter, and how can a husband help his wife cope? For the purpose of this book, we emphasize how a husband helps his wife release the pressures brought on by life. By inference, a husband will also find personal advice to assist him in coping with life's pressures.

In every person's life, situations happen that create pressures within that individual. Each person handles stressful moments in their own way. Some situations get to the husband, and the same event is sloughed off by his wife as nothing at all. Then she will become all tense over a specific event that the husband can breeze through without so much as a minor speed bump.

Why is it that each person handles situations differently? What are some of the specific circumstances that haunt husbands and yet do not seem to affect the wife in the least? For instance men have a difficult time asking for directions where women will seek help. Men seem to make it an ego issue which assaults their manhood that they are lost. Women look at this predicament and slough it off to solve the problem "We are lost!" On the other side women are more fixated on their appearance than men. If you notice your wife will speak about her clothes, her hair or how either is suited for the day or night time activity. You are most likely less concerned with your appearance than what is on the to-do list. These illustrations spring from deep inside yet each gender typically reacts to these life situations unlike the other. What situations or issues bother your wife that you allow to just slide by? What is stressful to your wife and how is stress created within your marriage?

Stress is that tension created in life from real or imagined issues that occur. These tensions build because a person did something wrong, or they can occur because of someone else's action and through no self-induced intentional action. Is your home a haven, or does each day create a more stressful environment after you arrive home? Is there a stress-relief valve or a way to eliminate stress each day? Let's see what produces our apprehensions and how to resolve those issues before they split your relationship.

Each Individual Brings a Set of Quirks to the Marriage

When two individuals combine to form a new household, some natural tensions will occur. No matter how well prepared a person is for this new setting, some tensions are unavoidable. Many times, these stressors are not formed out of any wrong intentions or habits. Here are a few instances couples can relate to:

- While he was growing up, the husband's **mother** prepared homemade biscuits every day for the family. Conversely, the wife's **father** always prepared breakfast for his family since he was a stay-at-home dad. See how these differences would create a tense situation each morning due to their expectations from growing up? Since **her father** did what **his mother** did each Sunday, they expected their partner to do the same for them. The problem is they assumed this was the "NORMAL" way breakfast was done in every home. So, how come he/she was not up fixing breakfast!?

- **Her** mother always put the socks in a basket after washing the clothes and did not put them into a dresser at all. **His** mother always folded the socks together and placed them in a basket for him to put away in his dresser drawer. Hmmm, could these differences create any stress? Many times, small habits form in life which people take for granted, assuming that "everybody" does it that way, when in reality, other households employ different methods for doing the same household chores.

- **His** mother picked up his clothes and placed them into the clothes hamper off the floor, where he was allowed to throw them after his shower. **Her** mother insisted that each family member deposit their dirty clothes into the hamper or basket after they showered. Do you think there might be an issue here?

A simple issue if it is resolved in the marriage early on can be a blessing. Unresolved, this same issue can fester for years. What were the differences growing up have that may have created a few tense moments when you first "set up house"?

Some more illustrations could be generated about how family upbringing creates its own set of uncomfortable situations in marriage. Situations like those mentioned above, if not handled before marriage, will create some "testy" situations when a couple first settles in together. These brief situations listed are real-life circumstances discussed among couples we have worked with at our marriage seminars. The attendees generated them to help each partner learn how to deal with family habits that created sensitive issues within their home.

It is always interesting to spend a few moments with couples who open up for discussion over issues like those listed above. Invariably these couples encountered family differences early in their marriage that they learned to overcome to arrive at a peaceful solution. When the couples chat about these incidents, it is frequently lighthearted as they share personal stories and everyone gets a good laugh about such times. However, when these small differences were first encountered, they created minutes or even days of distress between the couple. In these particular incidents, the problems were more often family customs than being an absolute moral right or wrong. They are simply how a certain family functioned. It may seem that, since one parent "always" did it that way, that made it right. Yet when they each step back from the sensitive personalities that are natural in these conversations, better discussions occur in the home. It is much like the difference between fact and opinion. One person's fact is often the other person's opinion.

As parents of grown children, it has been curious to witness these different ebb and flow situations in our children's homes. We are quick to remind them that just because mom or dad did it a certain way, it does not need to be law in their house. Developing peace within is far more important that keeping a certain personal habit from generation to generation.

Whenever a couple first moves in together, they bring certain "emotional baggage" since they are blending two diverse family backgrounds with opposing habits and values. It is not simply two individuals sharing a house together. Within a marriage, each partner comes to this new opportunity with his or her own pre-conceived ideas of what is "right" and "wrong" (often built upon how *MY* mom or dad did it when I was growing up). If a person lived a sheltered life, this often creates a stronger line of *"The right way "* to do a certain action in the new home. Heated misunderstandings can be avoided by having a specific conversation where each spouse contributes to the conversation about domestic habits growing up concerning what "your mom did for your dad and your dad did for your mom."

Dating Time Does Not Reveal All the Stressful Issues WHich Will Occur throughout your marriage

No matter how long a couple dates prior to marriage, within the first few years, they most likely will find many "hidden" traits of their spouse. It is not that she or he is hiding these particular behaviors. Intimate circumstances come to the surface as two individuals are together all the time. Take notice that some of those cute little quirks that the husband found so captivating when they were dating, seem to irritate him now. Why is it that small gestures at one time were special or "cute," and after a short time, these same actions become an aggravation?

Sometimes, a person is not acutely aware that a habit by their wife is becoming an irritant. Perhaps she has not told him she would like for him to do . . . ? Because of a question raised by another author, I asked Elaine one day, "What is a habit I have or do that you wish I did not do?" Of course, since we have been married for so many years, I thought she would say, "I can't think of any at this time." But she surprised me **and very quickly** replied, "I would like it if you didn't leave partially used tissues laying around." WOW! Was I caught off guard. However, I do not leave any tissues laying around now or partially soiled napkins either. I did not purposely try to offend my wife; I just wanted to use all the tissue before I disposed of it. At least that was the justification for my habit.

This habit had an easy fix. She is happier, and I know I am doing something that makes her life more contented. I plan on asking some form of this question a few times a year to keep working to be a better husband. Elaine never mentioned the tissue habit to me before, and of course, she did not nag me about it, so I was unaware of the problem. Even after forty years together, couples can learn new preferences about each other as husband and wife.

Here's a few typical problems couples face within their marriage. These problems do not just add up; they compound the harmful stress of a marriage

Jam-Packed Schedules Create Stress

Too often married couples find that the weeks get crammed with busy workloads. The daily "To-Do" lists fill to overflowing. People strive to accomplish more and more, and therefore, they have little time for those persons who should matter most, the wife and family. Too often, men justify their hectic schedules with the adage, "I am giving them what they want and deserve!" In reality, most surveys have shown that many wives and most children value the husband and father's *time* spent with them more than having a few additional toys or a bigger house. Too many couples are broken apart by the appetite for a better lifestyle.

Isn't it amazing that technology was supposed to generate more leisure time for people? Look at articles written prior to 1970. The technology on the horizon back then was supposed to create a three-day workweek with two months of pure vacation time! Oh well, so much for prognosticators!

Married couples feel that they are on a chaotic treadmill, working more yet achieving less value? Everyone tries to squeeze a bit more into their week, only to find that it oozes over into the next one. Workers tend to take on more projects to make someone else happy, while their family suffers. **Be careful not to sacrifice the family on the altar of work.** Certainly, weekly schedules can become a severe source of added tensions.

Kids Create Stress

Our three wonderful children are and were a delight growing up. But during those early years, our days were filled to the top with school and community activities. They did well in school but went several different directions because each one had their own set of interests. Sports, clubs, and after school interests all created a different set of tensions for mom in one way and dad in another. These all had to be integrated between jobs and marriage.

Many years ago as a couple, we developed a date night since our schedules with the kids became so demanding and we needed "us" time. When the kids were going through school it seemed to be a constant effort to stay on the schedule for the week or month. Then one day, we noticed we were empty nesters! Where did the years go? As we look back, we have many fond memories and no regrets for the time invested in our children. However, this time did not seem to take years; it went by in a flash.

The best advice for new parents is to enjoy the time through each new segment of family life. Initially, parents work to train their children to walk and talk and learn all the personal skills necessary to be an independent person. Quickly, these toddlers grow up and start school, and then the homework and afterschool activities crowd each day. It becomes a whirlwind to fit meetings and programs into the already hectic work schedules. But someday each couple can fondly remember many chorus, band, and sports tournaments where they drove several hours to watch the "best" parts happen, which involve their kids. Memories are rich when mom and dad take the time to be *with* their children.

This advice comes from two perspectives, one as a parent and the second one as a son growing up. Viewing my childhood, not all my memories about extracurricular activities were so fond. On the heartwarming side, my mom never missed any of my school or additional non-school events. My dad however, never saw any of my baseball or football games or band performances. I relate this because, as an adult, I still painfully remember wishing my dad had made the effort to be in the stands and watch these activities. Especially as a parent, I appreciate the sacrifices my mom made for me. It was always special to know whatever I did, she was there cheering me on and being proud of my accomplishments.

Make the time to be as involved as possible with your children. The momentary sacrifices are well worth the required effort. Children are only that certain age one time. They grow up too quickly. You can never get those times back. Children are an asset to a home. Invest in those assets as a couple, since a person cannot go back to regain those memories. Someone will get the work deadline finished, but seeing a child achieve a personal goal on a stage or field cannot be duplicated. Live with memories, not regrets.

Money Issues Create Stress

Dave Ramsey (www.daveramsey.com) makes the point frequently that financial problems are *the number one reason given for divorce in America.* How a husband and his wife deal with their finances is a critical ingredient to their marriage success. Are all the decisions shared equally about the money that comes into the home and where it is spent, no matter which person generates that money?

Too often, one partner will assume the responsibility for the checkbook and the budgeting of the money while the other spouse is oblivious to what happens in the household. That presents its own set of problems since they formed a joint partnership between a man and a woman. There are numerous horror stories about a couple going bankrupt and one spouse not being aware the marriage had any financial problems. One partner had no idea that they were heavily in debt until their debt was huge. Being incredibly in debt is not a time to assess blame since each spouse is as accountable as the other for their present condition. There are some very easy steps to ensure that a marriage avoids financial trauma. This home should be jointly monitored with shared responsibilities, especially when it comes to money. Because of following Dave's program through our seminars or directly at "Financial Peace University," couples "find" money they did not know they had.

One of the most important facts about a married couples finances is found in this next paragraph so read the next section very carefully.

Every married couple needs to have a written budget where every dollar is given a designation (a name) where it is going before the money gets into the checking account. Usually one spouse is better at managing the financial accounts than is the other. This personal talent does not absolve the first partner of the responsibility for knowing where each dollar is going to be spent before the month begins. Each marriage partner has an equal say in where the money is spent. They equally share the responsibility to oversee how the money is being spent.

At best once a month, or at worst every other month, a financial meeting needs to happen between the husband and his wife so there are no major surprises. It should be calculated how much money is coming in and how much is going out to pay the bills? The difference should be reflected in the checking and savings account. Money is one of those very sensitive issues that will break a marriage if not handled very respectfully. If either partner does not know how the money is being spent this month, arrange a meeting to discuss personal finances.

If a couple is not sure how to set a working budget for each month, seek help from a person who has become debt free. There is no shame is being in debt. Staying in debt or getting deeper into debt is the dangerous issue. In getting out of debt, seek help from people who are debt free, and do not listen to friends who are still trying to figure how in the world they got in such a mess themselves. There are people who really know how to help couples become debt free. Look at the websites at the back of the book under "Finances" to see who can be trusted. Becoming debt free is a glorious feeling like a giant weight has been lifted from the marriage.

Along with being strapped with debt, a couple can develop a dangerous mindset about whose money is whose. Each marriage should have one checking account for the family's money. Do not have "his and her" separate accounts. A Biblical marriage is one wife and one husband for life. Whenever a couple has separate checking accounts, they tend to look at the money as "his" and "hers" rather than "ours." Most financial advisors encourage couples to change that situation immediately. The marriage was performed to form one home. There might be slight exceptions to this rule, but until the money is in one account, it can fabricate some pressure-laden issues that need not exist. Don't allow the number one divorce issues in America to ruin a vibrant marriage.

Each Partner's Job Concerns Create Stress

Do both spouses work? A problematic concern about jobs is that people often feel their personal job is the more important one in the marriage. It does not need to be this way. Both spouses are distinctive, so their type of work and their pay structure will be different. How much each person generates is actually irrelevant in this part of the discussion. Both incomes create **one pile of money**.

Most men place a higher value on their self-worth based on the type of job they have and the pay they receive. The stark reality is that your job will be done by someone else when you are no longer at that particular job. What matters personally is that the family is cared for as best a person can provide at whatever job they can do.

If the wife works, she probably does not give the same level of emotional baggage to her job as he does to his job. For many women, it is a means to an end to help support the family. It is usually not her life or how she receives her self-worth. Yes, working is important and even satisfying to her, but her self-worth comes from relationships and not usually from having particular job skills. With every generality, there are exceptions, so be sure that both partners are honest in their vocational assessment as it relates to the home. The importance placed on jobs and their relative importance to the family as a whole is not fully interconnected. How often do couples change jobs in their lifetime? A job is just that, a job.

To clarify job responsibility and to avoid these situations from becoming a deal breaker for your marriage, discuss the following questions:

- If either partner were to be transferred, how would that affect the other spouse?

- What if one were asked to take a different position for less pay with more time to be at home, how would that impact the situation?

- What if either person were laid off for a few months, what should the couple do?

- If either person wants to quit their job to go back to school to become better prepared for another position, what are their feelings about that change?

- If children come into the picture, is the household financially ready? If not, how will it get better prepared? (By the way, couples never have enough money to "have children." This question is to help clarify where each spouse views children fitting into the situation.)

- Is each spouse presently where they want to be professionally? What changes would or should be made?

These are some quick thoughts to help a couple define their work-related objectives. Combined job schedules and individual identities can present their own set of strains upon the marriage.

Hobbies Create Stress

Hobbies seem to be a free-flowing subject, and yet for some couples, this can become a deal breaker. The problems arise when one partner thinks they will change the other spouse after they get married by getting their spouse to forsake the preferred hobby or leisure activity. Trying to change another person for any reason frequently goes poorly for both spouses. The one trying to be changed is resistant because they see no worthwhile reason to change.

The one who initiates the change does not understand why their spouse would be so stubborn and not want to conform to the wishes for the one they say they love.

Most likely, each spouse knew their partner's major interests prior to marriage. Why not enjoy these differences? Try to appreciate your spouse's special leisure pursuit.

My wife did not understand or appreciate my passion for football. I enjoy this sport at every level. Instead of allowing it to become a major problem early in our marriage, she sat next to me, and together we discussed the game. After a while, she became proficient in the major flow of the game.

Actually, at one point in a discussion between a few folks, one friend asked a question about a particular player, and Elaine answered the question before I did. The guy was so impressed and muttered, "I wish my wife knew something about football or enjoyed it with me." Elaine still does not have the same enthusiasm about football as me, yet we share this hobby in common because she took the initiative to learn about something I enjoy.

As for Elaine, her passion is sewing. She is a wonderful seamstress who can do an incredible job with very expensive dresses. She can take a luxurious bridal gown all apart and put it back together so that no one knew it was ever altered. For many years, she thought it was no big deal to rip these gowns apart and properly fit them back together again. She would say, "after all, anyone can sew!" I have been her biggest fan and brag to anyone who will listen about her expertise. She thoroughly enjoys sewing, and that has become her job as well. Often, when we are at a local restaurant, some high school girls come by in their "prom gowns," and I ask if she recognizes any of them? We discuss the type and colors, and I can tell you I am honestly interested in her work, even if I do not appreciate every detail of these dresses the way she does. This generates a warm flow of conversation as she relates some detail about how the dress is constructed or needed a particular alteration.

Reading is her second passion. One year, I gave her an electronic reader so she did not have to always go to the library or discount bookstore to pick up new books. There are many sites to download free books to read while we sit together in the living room. Another dynamic to the electronic reader is the ability to "surf the net," to look at other sites and view what our kids share about the grandkids online while sitting in the living room. We both unwind in our own way. It is a win-win! Learn to appreciate each other's hobbies, as it will draw each closer to the other.

Friends Create Stress

Some of the "baggage" a person brings to the marriage is their friends. Can a husband like his wife's friends? Does she like his friends? This can draw a couple closer together, or it can push them further apart.

If a husband is not fond of her friends, he can seek to find something in common with them for his wife's sake. He can establish peace about her friends and not promote a separation between his wife and her friends.

Likewise, he should not spend so much time with his buddies that his wife makes some remark such as, "You should have married them instead of me!" That is a huge warning sign and not one that needs to be negatively reacted to, nor should the comment be simply ignored. Yes, he should be able to spend time with friends. He may have known some friends longer than he has known his wife. However, he chose her to marry and not them. Especially in the beginning of their marriage, she wants to feel secure in the marriage relationship. He can enjoy his friends, and he should encourage his wife to do the same for her acquaintances.

What most couples discover after being married several years is they develop a new set of friends as a couple with other couples. These new couples will generally be their same age and be in a similar family relationship. It does not mean either spouse will not have any single friends after they get married. This is one area where they need to "go with the flow" and not create any big waves. Time has a way of allowing marriages to grow in their own directions as it relates to friendships.

Family: Each Set of In-laws Create Stress

This is sometimes one sided since one set of the in-laws can be more comfortable to be around than the other set. However, be cautious since each person naturally feels protective of their own parents. The husband might see his mother or father's personal issues, yet they are still his parents. Her parents are her mother and father, and no matter what problems he sees in them, he cannot harp about those problems to his wife, as she will defend her parents.

The best action to take is to warmly welcome each set of in-laws into the home as often as possible. These two sets of parents share one thing in common: their daughter and son, who are married to one another. Find ways to offer sincere compliments about each other's parents. Do not get caught up in bashing them like so many jokes that are told about in-laws. Due to the sensitivity here, remember they are each one's parents no matter what each partner thinks about them. Give them honor as parents. After all, they produced you two!

These Stressors Do Not Appear One at a Time

Each of these situations mentioned can produce their own set of problems all by themselves. Combine any two or more together, and the stress levels multiply. How are these negative situations defused in a relationship?

What is the Best Way Handle Stress that Threatens the Marriage?

Men and women react differently to pressures brought on by life. Men tend to "decompress" in silence or seek to be all alone because of their day's tensions. Women often want to interact and tell all the details of their pressure-ridden day. Does there seem to be any built in troubles if they each seek to have their own problems solved first upon arrival at home after a trying day? She wants to talk for a while, and all he wants to do is crawl off into his "cave" and unwind without any human interaction. Hmmmmm, there might be another dilemma brewing there?

Stress Happens when Opposing Emotional Worlds Collide

Before they get into conflicting life situations, where she wants to go one way and he another, they need to discuss this different set of stress issues when their life is at a calm state.

He should relate how important it is to have some time alone to unwind when he initially arrives at home. Some people call this a man's "cave time." Some men need time to "go to their cave" for a set amount of time, say fifteen or twenty minutes. Be sure to discuss this subject when life is not so hectic. Be cautions that this does not just become an excuse to not be fully engaged and present upon arrival at home. It should be the exception and not the normal fashion when he gets home. She deserves his attention when they initially see each other. However, some times, life gets to men so much that they need time alone before being civil.

There are a few creative ways to address this problem for him to decompress after his workday, depending on the physical circumstances. Pick from these workable settings. Perhaps join two of these ideas together or come up with some other thoughts based on these views.

Let's begin with the assumption that both partners had a bad day and really need each other's understanding. If they both arrive at the same time, how is the impending difference resolved?

1 – He will not get his "cave" time upon first entering the house, so he must find a suitable place to unwind for a few minutes on the way home. When he does this, it is important to let his wife know he will not arrive home at the normal time. This alerts her that he is sensitive to her feelings and will be willing to hear all about her day when his arrival at home.

Consider stopping at a park or favorite coffee shop and get something quick and take a walk around the parking lot to let off some "steam." Perhaps just stop at a parking lot and catch a quick nap or relax and listen to some music for a few moments. Each person needs to do something a bit out of the ordinary work crush to unwind. A spiritually minded person might pause to read through a favorite Bible section. Whatever it takes for a break of a few (and just a few) minutes to refocus and refresh before getting home will be beneficial for relaxation before getting home. Even if it takes some time to experiment a bit, find a way to get the day's business set aside to greet the family as if it were the best day of your life.

After just a few minutes to gain the necessary "sanity," continue the journey home. Think about the blessings of being married and having someone to come home to each day. As a polite gesture, send her a text to let her know the probable arrival time. In the text, let her know you are looking forward to hearing all about her day!

2 – Are there children at home the wife has dealt with all day? Assure her that you will take care of the kids upon arrival at home. After supper and the kids are down for

the night, spend time listening all about her day and its disasters. Just sit and listen to her as she verbally unpacks her day. Not sure exactly how to "just listen," go back through chapter five about "*Heartfelt listening to your spouse*."

3 – This should be a situation that **seldom arises**. Let's say that this particular day was very intense, so before addressing any of the issues the wife has faced, cave time is "genuinely" necessary upon initially getting home. Text or call to alert her to what type of awful day this has been. Before hearing how her day went, he needs time to chill out and then help her however she needs to have help. This should be a quick time out from the normal attention to her needs upon initial arrival home. If she is normally the one to fix supper, ask her how she needs help, and joyfully lend a hand. This can be compounded when children are present so it makes the arrival home a bit more important to be available physically and mentally. That is why in number one, it is suggested to take a short break prior to arrival to release this pressure. This is not an hour-long stop with the guys. It is a very short distraction to leave the stresses of work outside the home environment. Keep in mind that the children and wife did nothing to contribute to the disaster of a day. They want to see their daddy and husband and are eager for him to be home.

The main reason for these suggestions is to give a formula for how to be cheerful upon arriving home. Some couples get home and almost "throw up" on their spouse? What have they done to deserve this behavior? This is not a storybook type of dream. It is giving the best to this woman who committed to share her life with you.

Is it Time to Create This New Tradition at Home?

Create a new family tradition if this is not already somewhat like your entrance at home. Greet her with a 10–15 second romantic kiss and a long warm hug. This kiss is not to be the classic peck to politely greet her as a glancing blow on the way to another room of the house. Make every arrival home one that is looked forward to each day.

Be happy to greet your wife cheerfully, no matter who gets home first. *Always* greet and kiss your wife **before** giving any meaningful attention to the kids. If they rush to greet you at the door, gently let them know that "mom" gets the first kiss, and only then play and hear how their day went.

If there are children at home, after the loving embrace mentioned above, spend some time reconnecting with them. Stay engaged in their discussion about school or play time. Dads too often want the initial time at home to be away from the children to wind down from the workload of the day. Kids need to be with their dad.

At supper, be sure there are no distractions that take away from the family activities. The sooner you establish a policy of "no electronic devices to invade your supper table," the sooner the family can authentically connect each day. Even if there are no children, be sure to focus on your wife and enjoy this special time together.

Commercials today reveal that families are sidetracked by electronics that are allowed to intrude into the home too often. A family cannot become personally interconnected if additional sources of distraction are allowed to pry them apart. Spend the time discussing how each person spent their day. Make this a way for the family to feel safe and connected.

The Most Important Times of the Day

The last five minutes before each person leaves the house and the first five minutes after each person greets one another again are vitally important within the family relationship. The first five minutes upon your arrival can create a tone for the rest of the night. Keep in mind that one of those parting times will be the last. Ensure that every possible memory is the best a person can develop.

Find a Way to Release the Pressures of Life Through Shared Hobbies or Mutual Relaxing Activities

What hobby or recreational activity could be shared? Is there something enjoyable that is completely different than the job? If not, develop some shared activities: golf, softball, basketball, volleyball, etc. These can help release some of the pent-up pressures experienced throughout the week. Many companies encourage physical exertion for their workers, as these generate benefits beyond the positives of cardio exercise. Walking or biking has its recreational advantages with low stress on the limbs.

The best possible solution includes both husband and wife in these activities. When joined together, a physical hobby and personal interactions for both husband and wife will receive more than double the benefit. These pleasurable actions add significantly to the entire marriage environment.

Remember that when doing any physical activity, along with sexual activities, both partners will burn calories and enjoy the intimacy developed. Physical exertion will also develop a couple's friendly closeness. Ask her some of the high points from the marriage so far, and she might list some non-stressful activities she enjoyed where it was just the two of you, which may have slipped your mind. If any patterns emerge, think of how to create some more of those cherished memories in the near future together.

Here are some "bullet points" about relieving stress in a marriage (most articles have these in common):

- Get enough sleep

- Eat correct foods

- Get some sort of physical activity (keep it age and health specific; so avoid a marathon if there has been no running training lately)

- Connect often with those who matter most

- When a person feels ill at all, do not ignore those warning signs

- In this busy world, find some way to fully relax

- Learn to "detoxify" your entire life – financial debt and time management, along with increasing healthy relationships so far as it depends on you

- Seek to enjoy the important things, as the old adage is true: "You only go around once in life."

The relationship is the most important part of managing the pressures that occupy any person's life. As a married couple, helping each other learn how to handle the demands life throws at them is a rewarding yet continuous effort. Determine numerous ways to cope with all the daily burdens, and also learn how to assist your wife in continual healing.

Just prior to leaving home and first arriving back together are the two most critical times for marriage. Here are some PEP PILLS to help a couple de-stress and learn how to stay happy together!

PEP PILLS for Defusing the Time Bombs in

Marriage: Action Steps for a Better Marriage Relationship

 # 1 – Ask her what she sees as some potential stressful circumstances in your present relationship that needs to be addressed or eliminated? When your wife helps you find problems in your life be sure to make a personal list of these potential stressful areas as well. If she mentions anything that presents a problem that seems difficult to resolve, note it, and bring it up again once there is a chance to further investigate the facts so you can resolve the situation. Sincerely thank her for pointing out particular negative behaviors she sees with you.

 # 2 – Be willing to admit that personal opinions are not always fact – Make some suggestions where the two personal backgrounds have created some potential hot spots. Be the first to admit some of the individual family differences that have become apparent through this exercise. Be quick to point out a possible workable solution to resolving these differences. These differences are not as important as is the marriage. Most of these opinions are simply that, "opinions" – just how one person observes a situation, which is not how the other person views the same situation.

 # 3 – Ask your wife what additional habits have caused her discomfort or tension – Very often a person is not aware of a habit they have that might agitate the spouse. If she mentions something and it was not apparent that this "habit" bothered her, work to resolve the habit quickly. Through many years together, couples still learn new thoughts about each other. Sharing a life together is more fun than fussing about it!

 # 4 – Spend a minimum of twice a month on a date together for the purpose of staying present with each other – Dating without kids or other couples each week has several rewards for enhancing the marriage and keeping it fresh. This does not always mean expensive dinners or fancy, involved arrangements. Some of the most memorable dates through the years were just spending time with each other sharing a cup of coffee, with excellent communication about where life was at the moment and perhaps where it should go in the future.

Time alone away from all the normal hectic life situations generates a wholesome emotional reconnection process. No specific agendas or certain line items are needed for these personal interludes. Just enjoy being together, and bask in the moment. Stress can destroy a relationship if left unchecked. Make the efforts necessary to create lasting memories. In the next chapter, learn how to turn these date nights into an all-day romantic interlude getting prepared for some sparks to fly!

Always expect the best for your marriage!

CHAPTER 7

Breathing Nourishing Romance Into Your Marriage

Romance in its most practical form is doing small acts of kindness for another person with no strings attached. The problem for most married couples is that men and women envision romance very differently.

This could be the most important chapter in *any book* to help marriages flourish and not simply survive! The force behind that statement is because too many couples erect a dividing wall between each other concerning their wholesome nurturing romantic life. Romance is the "linchpin" that all the other parts a marriage pivot upon. Follow and implement what is found in this chapter correctly and any marriage will grow naturally, beginning from enhanced verbal communication skills through to regular pleasurable sexual fulfillment. When romance is approached incorrectly, every clueless husband wonders why his attempts at romance unhappily deteriorate and his wife does not open up the way many of the step-by-step "manuals" propose.

Her frustration arises as she does not know to instruct him as to how to treat her differently. Romance is second nature for her, but he seems clueless. Many wives feel that if they have to tell him what they really need, it loses the enticing edge for them.

Learning How to be Romantic for Your Wife, Might be Like Teaching a Clumsy Child How to Run Smoothly

Effectively cultivating the ideal performance of a new talent takes time and practice developed by a skilled coach. A husband has all the tools to become a highly romantic husband. The problem is that many husbands have listened to the wrong "coach" for their guidance, such as the media or pornography. Here, we will provide the right coaching.

Here is a personal application of a different experience for clarification to show the value of coaching. Around eleven years old, my brother grew at an incredible rate, as kids often do at that age. By the sixth grade, he was nearly six feet tall. When a child grows faster than their reflexes can keep up, he outgrew his sense of balance and steadiness. Raymond was a big, lumbering kid who, when taunted by me, could not catch me. I was still quick and agile. Then Ray started playing organized tackle football. Then something amazing happened, which I did not immediately notice. Gradually, these coaches taught my brother to harness his size and muscular agility. One fateful day, as I had often done on prior occasions, I taunted Ray and darted away. Then it happened, he caught me! I could not escape his powerful grasp. From that experience, I learned a great lesson (well several life lessons actually): life has its way of leveling the playing field. This clumsy giant (at least for me at barely four feet tall) who was now an athlete, did not stay a clumsy kid. Ray became a gifted athlete who learned how to retrain his body and turn a negative situation into a productive process. He had this proficiency all along, yet it took a proper coach's time and effort to help my brother become an athlete. The byproduct of this physical prowess was an internal confidence.

What my brother learned in a physical and an emotional sense from training his physical body is what any husband can learn in the field of romance within their marriage. A husband can train himself to become whatever his wife needs concerning wholesome romance. Proper coaching + a willing student = effective outcome (a husband who understands and applies the romantic needs of his wife).

This chapter could be called: "Clueless husband needs a makeover!"

That caption is too blunt, even though it may indicate a glaring problem. Here in Chapter Seven, both sides of this romance dilemma will be resolved when these romantic actions are put into practice. So, let's start with the basics and work through the maze that is a woman's emotional mind and heart.

Romance is not a mathematical equation

Because of a man's God-given inner design, they are focused on an "action/reaction" foundation for much of their thinking. Men tend to see a problem and determine what action will solve the difficulty. So, when a husband sees an issue in a relationship, he tends to resort to "problem-solving" mode with his wife. Hence, his conflicting predicament is that romance is not a mathematical problem. The issue is not so much the process as it the misunderstanding of his "subject," his wife, who is a woman. Wrapping his mind around the inner workings of wholesome romance within the body of a woman is incredibly different than romance inside a man's mind. DUH!

Hang in there a bit as we peel back the male reasons for initiating romantic activities with his wife and then dig into romance from a woman's perspective. **Scary, but workable!** Fortunately, this examination will set the tone for active, lively signals that nourish the kind gesture any wife hungers for. In reality, this is an enjoyable journey. REALLY, it is. We will generate some specific techniques to personally tweak and fit your wife's unique personality.

Husbands learn this: **romantic gestures are NOT accumulations of specific performed activities to ensure a specified desired result – SEX.** Too many husbands believe that giving their wife flowers will get their wife to have sex with them.

What Do Husbands Actually Want To *Get* From Their Romantic Actions With Their Wife?

Why do husbands perform any romantic actions for their wife? Honestly, it is so their wife will get sexually turned on for them. This may be a bit blunt, but many husbands look at romance as a blatant ploy to get their wife to do what they want. When she senses this as his motive, it creates a feeling that she is an object being maneuvered in a preset direction, towards the bed. Women do not appreciate being **pushed** in any direction. Deep down, she may know he is attempting to meet her needs as the person he cherishes and knows her husband loves her, yet he does not effectively provide the romance she needs, so the wife feels used instead of being loved. Since she feels manipulated for his pleasures instead of being nurtured towards a romantic interlude, the husband hears his wife express, "You just don't understand me!" Helping a husband understand how his wife reacts to this typical male treatment of unromantic actions, confirms what the genuine acts of kindness (romance) are designed to accomplish.

To fully understand this "push" principle, view this unintentional manipulation from the other side. What if his wife did various practices to merely get him to work harder at his job or to get some project accomplished around the house for her? What if he knew her entire reason for cooking a special meal or doing any other "chore," was to drive him harder in a specific direction that suited her selfish needs? He would resent that treatment, right? How often have wives said to their husband, "If you do this . . . you might get lucky tonight?" While having sex is good, this husband probably thought, "So why is it she will not initiate sex with me when she doesn't need for me to get some job done?"

True Romance is to Pull the Heart, Not To Push the Will

For either the husband or the wife, romance is not an act of manipulation to get some designed response from the wife or from the husband in return for their doing some desired activity. The entire reason for the thoughtful treatment by the husband for his bride should be to encourage her heart because he wants her to know he cares for her, with no strings attached. In the next chapter, we will cover how to create a clear signal that both spouses understand what leads to the desired sexual fulfillment.

For this chapter, think of romance as "pampering" her because she is the one who committed her life completely to you, providing some authentic thoughtful actions for the sole purpose of expressing to her that she is worthy of any affection and kind gestures offered. Romance is not a single act, nor a collection of actions strung together to simply get someone to perform an act for personal needs of any type. Instead, **consider romance as a lifetime series of activities where one spouse lavishes the other with reminders of their love and devotion.** These affectionate gestures need to become a lifestyle, not merely planned activities. Romance is the bonding agent that will cement wife and husband together emotionally and physically. Authentic romance will build many lasting shared memories.

Wholesome romance is not to drive a wife towards the bedroom.

Rather, it is to draw her towards to his heart.

Wives crave affection from their husband. His affection, physically, emotionally and verbally, may be her greatest emotional cravings. One way to help satisfy that need is through genuine actions that show her unconditional submission to her and her alone. This art of romance is more than any certain act accomplished. Romance is a lifestyle that involves learning a creative standard for loving one woman for life. It is not simply a series of activities to be performed on her. This thought is what inspired my initial blog, www.**CrackingTheRomanceCode.com/blog**. Romance is finding the continuous sequence of affirmative behaviors to provide her with the love she craves. This means the husband is to continually repeat to his wife his devotion to her alone. This serves as a gentle reminder that he enjoys being her partner through life.

> Dr. Willard Harley, Jr. says, "The typical wife doesn't understand her husband's deep need for sex any more than the typical husband understands his wife's deep need for affection." (Pg 49 – His Needs Her Needs, Fifteenth Anniversary Edition)

A wife needs affection as deeply as her husband needs sex. The unfortunate predicament is that neither person fully grasps the strength of this opposing emotional need in their spouse. It is not that she thinks kisses and hugs are nice, she **NEEDS THEM** to function every day. A wife naturally needs to feel secure in her marriage. A wife desires continuous reminders of her husband's total commitment to her as his bride. The longer they are married, the more she wants to hear "I love you!" If they continually develop their relationship through the years, there is no time she will get tired of hearing that he is focused on capturing her heart. When does a husband think he will want to stop having sex with her? Why are drugs for erectile dysfunction so often advertised and purchased? Because older men want to quit having sex? I didn't think so! Wives need continuous authentic affection to be ready for sex just as you need sex to feel affectionately bonded to her.

Wives Hunger After More Non-sexual Touching

God has so wired a woman that she needs continuous dedicated bursts of kindness. She needs attention through her husband's affection. Fellows, ever noticed how often she seeks out kisses? Does she like hugs? It is not a "showy" expression on her part to desire kisses and hugs. She wants to reaffirm her emotional connectedness with her husband. For a woman, affection is like comfortable "glue" that holds the marriage together.

In the marriage seminars, the attending wives often speak about "non-sexual touching." When husbands hear this phrase for the first time, they scrunch their face and look at their wife with a quizzical expression. This phrase seems foreign to most men, non-sexual . . . touching? Most of the husbands will remark in some fashion, "How do you touch intimately that is not sexually arousing?" So, I say to the husbands, "Ask your wife what she means by non-sexual touching." This generates new territory for these marriages to grow in an area they had not previously explored.

These wives have generated a list of suggestions, which are noted here. Take a few minutes after highlighting this list, to ask your wife if she agrees. (By the way, some of them are not exactly **physical touching**, but since the wives listed them as such, they are listed here.)

- ❖ Holding hands while driving, walking or sitting together, anywhere.

- ❖ Touching her arm, shoulder, or neck at anytime and often.

- ❖ Hugs whenever they come into close proximity or because he chose to go and give her a hug, "just to affirm he cares about her!"

- ❖ Making her a meal and serving it to her while she relaxes.

- ❖ Bringing her a gift when it is not a special day such as an anniversary, birthday, and so on: flowers, a greeting card to say he was thinking of her, her favorite candy or treat (one husband brings his wife her favorite coffee every so often).

- ❖ A text or a phone call to say "I am thinking about you." This is especially good if he is going to be late or if he stops at a store and asks if she needs something while he is there?

- ❖ A shoulder massage or rubbing a special sore spot, brought on by her particular type of work.

- ❖ Taking care of the children so she has some "time alone" to unwind.

- ❖ Taking a walk together (this is a good time to hold her hand).

What would your wife add to this list? Be sure to make a written note of her thoughts.

Any husband can learn to be romantic no matter his situation or emotional disposition in life at the moment. This physical attention will continually affirm that her husband enjoys reconnecting with her in a non-sexual fashion. Keep in mind that the purpose of these gestures is to tell your wife very clearly that you are happy that she is your bride. She longs for this affection. Artful affection shows your wife that you are delighted to be her husband.

Here Are Some *"**Real**"* Non-sexual Gestures:

- ✓ Pick up the dirty laundry, and then wash and dry them?

- ✓ Make sure the toilet seat is lowered. Men are notorious for this one. Ensure that your wife can't say that.

- ✓ Take out the trash. Also, on the correct day, take the cans out to the curb and retrieve them upon arriving home.

- ✓ Are there children in diapers? Change those things as often as they need to be changed. It does not make a husband less of a man to change stinky diapers!

- ✓ Do the dishes every so often. Enjoy the time together in the kitchen, or tell her to go relax, you have this! Wives love a man with dishpan hands. As Earl Wilson once said, "No woman has ever shot her husband while he was doing the dishes!" (It's a joke, son!)

- ✓ Look for jobs around the house that the wife normally gets stuck doing to help her out a bit. The *Husband's Handbook* does not give any husband the right to make his wife do every job around the house. (Psssst – there is no *Husbands Handbook*! – maybe that could be the name for this book. Hmmm.)

Here Are Some Extensive Date Ideas

In the "PEP PILLS" section at the end of the chapter, there are some ongoing easy activities to plan, which are simple to accomplish. However, here is a list of some more involved "dates" that people have shared with us or which we have experienced together as a couple. These suggestions, as opposed to the PEP PILLS, are more expensive and require more detailed planning to set the entire date. Be aware that the object of romance is to make your wife feel very special. She should think, "Wow, am I ever glad I married him!" So, let the more involved planning begin.

This event was a weeklong vacation designed by Elaine for me. After we sold our business, which I had developed for almost twenty years, I really needed some down time. She made all the plans and executed those strategies in a wonderful fashion. The company I sold my business to kept

A Trip to a Gatlinburg, TN Cabin

me on as a salesman/consultant. Elaine contacted my new boss and asked for the time off, which he granted. It turned out that we spent a week doing exactly what I needed, nothing much! We did a tour of the local sites, as much as were open during the winter months. The amusement parks in Gatlinburg, Tennessee, are closed for several months during the off-season. We enjoyed the local shops and restaurants and visited some friends who live near there. It was an extended trip, which showed her dedication and respect for my needs.

₰ Fun Scavenger Hunt in the Mall & Beyond

This is an idea devised for Elaine and adapted from several sources. The first step was to create an easy "logo" made out of a couple of hearts, a few special words printed on specific paper and on the corresponding envelopes. Next the number of stops that she was to enjoy was mapped out, along with what the end prize of the scavenger hunt would be. Then the particular stores were considered and the exact items she was to get in each store. At each stop, a note was included in a sealed envelope with directions for the next move and what to do there. Some envelopes contained money, while, at other stops, she only needed to pick up what was already purchased. At these stores, the sales lady behind the counter held the package, awaiting some woman to enter the store with the specific, secret, coded stationary to retrieve the items. The particular stores and the related merchandise gave small clues to our special date, but they did not indicate the complete end result. The stores ranged from bath and fragrance to lingerie, from candles to massage oils, and more. At each shop, the look on the clerks face was priceless as I explained what was going to happen in a short while. Elaine told me the sales ladies said they needed their husband to "take some lessons." While the words were nice, this was a special reminder to my wife just how precious she is.

The initial process began by sticking a note on her car mirror while she was in at work. A quick phone call about it in the afternoon told her a surprise awaited her in the car after work. Of course, the first note said to go into the mall to a specified counter and show the personal "logo" to the sales lady. Each lady enjoyed seeing Elaine come in finally, as they wanted to know what was going on and what this mystery woman looked like! As a side note, the clerks told Elaine it made their day just looking for this special secret woman to come into the store for this unique shopping experience. At the last store, Elaine was instructed to drive home and stay in the car in our driveway and wait for me.

She was told we were going out to eat and that the kids were cared for while we were away. While driving to the restaurant, she told me her reactions to the notes and to the different clerks. After dropping her at the door and parking the car, Elaine had been taken to her seat already. A bouquet of flowers which had been stashed in the back of the car were given to the hostess with the request that she bring them to our table in a particular amount of time. It was a lot of fun to watch everyone in the place watch the hostess walk past the tables and come to ours and present Elaine with the flowers. Of course, the note revealed who they were from and gave a hint as to the rest of the night, but still held out a few surprises.

After our meal, there was a quick drive across the highway to a hotel where we enjoyed a room reserved for the night. It was a very special time with many interesting memories. Personal perspectives from this event have been shared with many couples. Although this occurred many years ago, it was well worth the effort and a lot of fun for both of us!

A Thoughtful "Brick," Planned Many Years Ahead of the Unveiling

Whenever thoughtful romantic gestures come to mind, this story of two close friends of ours, Greg and Wendy, who had been married over twenty years at the time this event completely unfolded takes center stage. More than ten years prior to their twentieth anniversary, Greg had the idea of buying a custom-designed "brick" in Disneyworld, Orlando, Florida, to celebrate a wonderful occasion. This is no ordinary block of clay that lines the walkway at the "Magic Kingdom." It is inscribed with their names and the specific anniversary date carved upon it. Wendy caught wind that something special was taking place, but she was not sure precisely what was "that" special event. Nearing their special twentieth anniversary, Greg said that they were taking a trip to Florida. On the wonderful setting for the surprise to be revealed, Greg took her to Disneyworld and showed Wendy the brick where it was displayed for all the world to see. It took many years to pay for their special anniversary trip and of course to "unveil" the brick. He is one of my "romance" heroes!

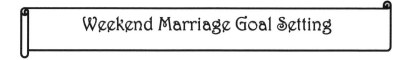

Weekend Marriage Goal Setting

Taking the necessary time all alone to focus on marriage is important. Plan a three-day hotel respite alone with no external distractions. Many marriage enrichment coaches recommend for couples to get away each year for the purpose of re-connecting and planning their next year together, and possibly the next five and ten years of marriage. This means that some additional plans are made for a goal-setting weekend, versus a "let's just getaway and veg" time. You certainly need to understand each other's agenda before you start planning this type of extended time out of the house. If you need additional help send me an email and request some suggestion about a get-a-way weekend - PepUpYourMarriage@hotmail.com

For this "goal-setting" three-day trip, have a specific set of questions to go through to emphasize where the present situation and where each partner expects to be in the next year, next five years, and next ten years. However, a bit of a caution before getting too involved in the planning stage for the trip, be sure to plan so there is ample free time to exchange ideas and dreams with each other in a relaxed fashion. Perhaps, leave the Friday night of the weekend to just dream weave during the travel to the hotel and during the leisurely supper.

Another caution for the first time on this type of relaxing/planning trip, keep in mind each other's personality when looking to discuss goals and dreams. Both spouses should come to the sessions with general thoughts as to what the future holds together as a couple. Whoever is the "nerd" might form some questions for mental digesting before actually arriving at the specific date mutually arranged for the getaway. If desired, purchase a set of DVDs or CDs from a speaker to generate a preset group of questions to follow. Create a personal recording prior to the weekend for this same purpose of setting an agenda to follow specified thoughts and questions and then mutually answer as it flows along as a couple. Generally, one partner will be better at keeping track of the thoughts generated and organizing these initial ideas into a new set of goals for the future. No matter the outcome, enjoy the planning time and whatever additional activities as a couple. This weekend is designed to invigorate a couple's spiritual and emotional batteries.

Several Creative Yet More Expensive Ideas

Here are some general ideas that are more expensive and a bit more involved to enjoy with your wife.

o Take a small plane ride. Many local airports have pilots that will give rides to see the town and house from the air. When a couple lives in a large city, the smaller airports in the outskirts of your city will provide guided tours in the surrounding countryside. No matter the trip, it could be a very romantic trip.

o Many areas are prime spots for going up in a hot air balloon. Pack a picnic basket and enjoy the countryside drifting along together through the clouds.
o More adventurous? Go skydiving or bungee jumping. While not for the faint of heart, these can create some wonderful memories.

o How about skiing? Either water or snow skiing can supply some wonderful new experiences.

o Most colleges have sports events to attend. Even when a couple did not attend the local school, the atmosphere for a game is very entertaining. The thrill of the crowd and the specific food there can create a nice change from the normal routine. Whenever possible, a favorite team located nearby makes a fun outing to go support them and perhaps go the night before and stay at a hotel!

o Go to a specific weekend event. What hobbies or special interests does your wife enjoy? Gardening? A specific craft? Take her to a show that specializes in that interest. Find out where they occur and how to get to them. Schedule some interesting restaurants along the route to and from the event. Locate the specific activities online, their dates, and what else is nearby. Planned correctly, these activities could become marriage highlights for years to come.

In all these extended "dates," relax, have fun and build memories, for that is the stuff that life is made from: shared memories. Some of these ideas can be planned early in a secretive fashion and some need to be shared due to scheduling conflicts. Always keep her interests at the forefront of these plans. What does she need and what does she want to do with her leisure time together? Don't get too hung up on making each date the "perfect" memory. Some of the best memories are "busted" dates or plans that went awry from the way they were first envisioned. The key point is to enjoy every moment possible with each other. Whenever these provide a great adventure, then that is a bonus. Enjoy the ride because the trip is always quicker than either person first thought it was going to be. Discuss the details about was enjoyed on the particular date and what was a bit lacking. Incorporate these newfound ideas into any future plans. Keep crating memories along the years of shared marriage enrichment.

PEP PILLS To Promote Additional Romance Into The Marriage: Action Steps For A Better Marriage Relationship

 # 1 – Plan a Distinctive Date Night once a month for the next twelve months. Cheerfully make all the details happen. Where does she enjoy going? Is there some restaurant that has been omitted lately? Perhaps there is some unknown establishment friends have said is really good? Call ahead to see what arrangements need to happen before arrival.

Here are some suggested basic details and ground rules to enhance the mood:

- No kids allowed. No cell phone on you, or if it necessary for an emergency at work, at least set it on vibrate. If she needs her phone for the kids in case of an emergency, then that should be OK.

- Declare prior to these date nights that these are purposely designed to indulge her desires.

- Search for feedback along the twelve dates schedule to ensure they meet the desired goal.

Be sure to create a loving set of guidelines that encourages affection. Being alone together is for the purpose of reconnecting with each other without interruptions. Perhaps have some brief and very general questions set aside to ask and get a good discussion started.

When appropriate, discuss some issues in the marriage that needs to be addressed. These questions are to open up a comfortable dialog. This is not a time to hash out complicated circumstances. Here are a few basic thoughts to help you get the discussion started; make them personal:

✓ Ask her what she needs to feel even more loved. Is there something from her perspective that could be done more often or something that needs to be discarded to confirm greater love for her?

✓ Ask what changes she would like to make to the house. Is there some project she has had in the back of her mind but just thought it would be too expensive or too time consuming?

✓ Is there something hidden from her that needs to be shared where she needs to extend forgiveness?

✓ Perhaps these dates are not the time to bring up "bombshells" within a relationship but rather to just give some intimate emotional contact not ordinarily covered.

And here are some additional things that you should remember to do on the date:

✓ On each date find **seven different areas** to sincerely compliment her. Look at her appearance and notice any subtle differences in her makeup or wardrobe. Does she dress in a more sexy fashion when these dates are planned? Be sure to focus even more on her when together.

✓ Express at least four times on every date that you love her. Ask her if love is expressed to her in enough different ways and as often as she needs for it to be expressed.

✓ Practice the lost art of chivalry: open her door; remover her coat gracefully; slide her chair in for her; notice if her drinking glass gets near empty, and ask the server to refill it!

 # 2 – Once every other week for the next 90 days give an inexpensive "gift" tailored just for her. Remember that pure romance is doing small acts of kindness for another person with no strings attached. Wholesome romance is not to push your wife towards the bedroom; it is rather to pull her towards your heart.

- It could be something as simple as getting her favorite candy bar with a nice handwritten note attached.

- Does she like candles or some sort of collectible items? When was the last time you stopped just to get her one or more small bits and pieces that she wants?

- How about her favorite gum? Get her several packs and sprinkle them in places she will find them throughout the weeks ahead. Perhaps attach smiley faces or hearts to them? Use these packs of gum to bring an added smile to her heart.

- Get a single rose with a few added smaller flowers in the bouquet in her favorite color.

- Bring an arrangement of "seasonal" flowers: fall = oranges and browns, summer = yellows and reds. Ask the florist or person at the local food store what is appropriate or special for that particular time of the year. Place a special card that lets her know she is remembered.

- Does she like animals? Get her some type of stuffed inexpensive dog or cat! Apply a lot of imagination as she is worth it.

Be sure to mark your smart phone or personal calendar as a reminder for these activities. Go ahead and select a gift each month and put it on the particular date to give her the present. Don't always give them the same day of the week or in the same fashion. Leave one on her pillow. Leave one in her car or her purse.

The actual cost of the gift is not *as **important*** as the thoughtfulness and creativity displayed. This gesture is to help her know someone sees her differences and appreciates her uniqueness.

Women really like it when their man does a bit extra to show her how much he cares for her. Have lots of fun with these PEP PILLS, keeping in mind that the target for all these gestures is to bring a huge smile to her heart!

Always expect the best for your marriage!

CHAPTER 8

Nine-to-Five Foreplay – Unraveling the Mystery for Men

"When is it Romance and when is it

Foreplay?"

Let's get something out in the open, in case any husband has been reading his wife's signals incorrectly: **She is a sexual being, and she enjoys sex!** God created her that way. She enjoys being sexual when she is ready to receive her husband emotionally and physically – in that order. However, a husband can help his wife bring out her sexual side in the fashion and speed she desires when he understands her needs. She does not get "turned on sexually" in the same way her husband gets turned on.

Foreplay and romance are separate entities welded together within the marriage bond. While romance may soften the wife's heart and allow her to accept her husband's foreplay, they are different in action and motivation. In chapter seven, it was pointed out that romance is the kind actions done by the husband because he loves and cherishes his wife, period. No sexual favors should be expected because he takes her to a movie, buys her flowers, or performs any gentle reminder that they are married and personally bound by sacred promises to her and her only as long as they both shall live.

Unravel the Mystery

So, how does a husband understand the difference between the last chapter on romance and this chapter on "Foreplay," since foreplay might employ some of the same activities or gestures as romance? **Ladies, please be patient; this is very confusing for guys!** Women have the ability to let ideas slide all around and cross each other in their mind. Men have a difficult time thinking about something that cannot fit neatly into only one "box" in their mind. So, romance and foreplay for men often get shoved into the same box if they are not careful, since many of the same activities for these two functions are not the same outcome.

Here is a confusing issue to consider. Holding his wife's hand is romantic, but the husband is not intending to get his wife sexually excited at this time. Yet holding her hand may create within her an excitement towards sex? When we point this out, some wives are saying, "Yes, that's correct," and their husbands are tilting his head and asking, "What????????" So it is time to examine this manly mystery, especially as it pertains to foreplay being different from romance. This chapter is about foreplay as its own entity. First, we will briefly explain the **motive** behind why a husband will engage in romantic interludes or frisky foreplay in the first place.

First, What Is *Foreplay*?

Foreplay is the ability for a husband to arouse his wife's senses before the actual "intimate, physical sex act" starts. It works as well for the wife to stimulate her husband. However, the most common circumstance involves the husband working to sexually stimulate his wife. That sounds so basic and even a bit clinical. And yet for men, it often seems elusive or slippery to comprehend if they are to engaged in romance or starting foreplay. This chapter is to help decipher these two concepts, which at times may seem a bit "scientific" and not sexy. Understand that romance is to create a warm emotional feeling with the wife as the end in itself. Foreplay has as its end result in sexual fulfillment.

Preparation for the main sexual activity must develop in his mind before he creates that environment for his wife. What does she need to be sexually aroused? Look at that question again. It does not ask, "How do most husbands approach their wife sexually?" Some men are curious as to why sometimes she is eager for them to bond sexually and yet these very same actions done on a different day cause her to close down and act like a porcupine with her barbs out fending him off.

Her sexual arousal cycle is completely different than his. Her methods for sexual arousal today might change tomorrow, or she might constantly change throughout the marriage one day to the next. Unless a husband stays hypersensitive to his wife's needs, he could miss out on many nights of intense sexual bliss because his arousal is foremost in his mind instead of her needs being met first.

Husbands: don't let this be you!

Sadly, some husbands view foreplay exclusively as a hurried system to push his wife towards sex. Too many husbands view foreplay as merely lasting a few minutes just prior to any actual sex activity. Perhaps, he looks at foreplay as how slowly he undresses his wife or picks out the correct mood music or candles while they are making love. Maybe he sees foreplay as those certain "moves" he makes to tell her he is "in the mood." Too often these moves take place a few minutes before bedtime as they turn off the computer or TV?

For most women, this is not the way they perceive loving foreplay between a woman and a man. The reason for this chapter's title, "**Nine To Five Foreplay**" is to emphasize that a wife needs extended sensuous stimulation during her entire day to be ready to enjoy the pleasures of sexual fulfillment with her husband. She would rather not be just groped or touched during the final minutes before jumping into bed. A wife wants to know that her husband cares about her and that he thinks about her in many ways during his day and not merely for sex at the end of the evening. If he is not careful, she could see herself as an object and not a beloved person.

If a husband is asking himself, "what does my wife consider sensuous foreplay?" instead he should ask her. Then be ready to hear that her needs change with the events surrounding her life. For a man, this could become challenging, since he becomes sexually stirred up very easily and often through the same stimulus. Women, however, are more complicated concerning sexual stimulation. One day, she is at peace and wants her husband without an increased amount of extensive sexual enticement. Another day, everything crashes in on her, and she needs compassionate understanding and abundant gentle stimulation to be prepared for their night together. It is best to determine her unique desires, rather than assuming he actually knows his wife and let her remain frustrated for many years.

As in all sections of the book, spend some time in personal discussion over her individual needs when it comes to foreplay. Highlight some paragraphs where each partner disagrees with the paragraph's information and ask her thoughts about a particular topic mentioned. This chapter emphasizes the brand of foreplay that most women seem to prefer in the "normal" ebb and flow of their particular hectic lifestyle. **A wise husband will ask his wife how she wants to be aroused by him in her perfect setting.** Determine what she wants and what she needs by seeking to fulfill her needs relative to these extended forms of stimulation for her pleasure.

In this chapter, a husband can find many forms of stimulation for his wife's pleasure. Adapt these techniques to fit your wife's individual mood and life experiences. Look at them as fun exercises and not as clinical school assignments.

Let's Begin this Wonderful Journey: All-Day Foreplay

From a woman's point of view, romantic stimulation should begin early in the day and continue throughout the day. This inconsistency in beliefs between husbands and wives has led to many illustrations for a man and a woman's sexual arousal comparisons. One simple suggestion showing the time necessary for adequate emotional and physical preparation is that she is like a "Crock-Pot" and he is like a "microwave." When God made male and female, it involved more than different male and female plumbing. He made male and female emotional wiring very different as well.

Certainly, there are some days when a wife is turned on in a much quicker time frame. It seems that most wives see this as the *rare occurrence* in the best of circumstances. For the purpose of this book, let's take the extended approach to foreplay, as most men already know how to take the quicker route to the "main course" sexually.

Men are usually aroused from the outside in: visual stimulants such as sight, sounds and smells can get him aroused in an instant.

Women are typically sexually aroused from the inside out: they prefer to have their mind and emotions stimulated first before their body can wholeheartedly join in.

There are some common misunderstood differences for men and women on this possible volatile issue. It is volatile because a man gets turned on sexually very quickly without much perceived stimulus. A woman typically gets sexually turned on very slowly. Since that is true for most wives, how should her husband work to fully serve his bride? Let's look at how to sexually fulfill a wife's desire in the way that she needs to be turned on to be ready for sexual fulfillment.

The purpose of foreplay is to build her anticipation of becoming sexually excited. Use this chapter as a guideline, not a schematic or step-by-step instructions to follow each time you want to be physically intimate with her. Learn to improvise, but always err on the extended amount of time in teasing foreplay rather than on the speedy side. "Quickie sex" certainly has its place in a marriage, yet this should be the extreme exception according to most wives and not the regular experience. Learn the "*ART*" of teasing in foreplay. Build desire and expectation for something more exciting to take place in the near future. Husbands, learn to use tension and anticipation to build up and tease your wife.

Become creative and playful while focusing on her specific needs. Remember that while a man is visual, a woman is verbal and emotional. Speaking kind, generous words of honest praise will awaken her softer side. Assuming a husband knows his wife will create a dangerous condition for him. Accurate knowledge will unlock the mysteries within his wife.

Think through these questions with her special needs in mind:

- Do you see her as a bride? If so, treat her like that beautiful person who pledged her life to you. Express to her every day that she is a bride.

- How spontaneous does she like foreplay? Is this spontaneity due to her desires or preconceived impressions of her needs?

- What does she really need to prepare sexually? Be sure that preparations actually reflect **her thinking** and not preconceived impressions about women in general. There is no other person just like her in the universe; she is one in seven billion! She has pledged her life, including her body, in marriage for you only. Treasure that exclusivity that she is presenting in the marriage bed.

- Be sure to dig deep enough and long enough to find out what this special woman genuinely needs to be ready for any or all sexual progress.

- In **her** "perfect" setting, starting with humdrum interests and progressing up to things that would highly excite her, what would she need as extended sexual stimulation? In this most important segment of mutual intimacy, there should never be a time for personal satisfaction placed above her ecstasy. Every sexual activity will not be equal in practice nor in sexual experience to other occurrences. However, the relationship will abound if her pleasure is uppermost in your mind.

Do Your "*Homework*"

Have you listened to what she says about her favorite books, movies, or TV shows?

Ask her about the main characters in these stories.

What qualities in the women does she really gush about, and what qualities does she like about the various men on the screen or in the books?

What words does she use to express how other husbands demonstrate kind and gentle actions to their wives?

Begin to pick up on the subtle ways she cares for children, not simply that she keeps   her own   kids fed and cleaned, although those are fine traits to praise about her. Does she create "works of art" with them?

Does she play at their level? Does she engage   them for new learning experiences?

These are wonderful loving gestures to store up in your mind to pay tribute to your wife. Become aware of the "little" things she does for the family that actually adds up to big benefits.

If this is a difficult list to create in your mind, "cheat" a bit. Ok, so it is not really *cheating*, it is receiving help in specific areas of her inner feelings. Investigate and determine creative ways to supplement this list.

- First, ask a couple of her close friends something they admire about her. Take note of their ideas and build on those suggestions. Be sure to share with those friends a couple of personal positive thoughts about her.

- Speak with her mom. What does she think are her daughter's most endearing qualities?

- Perhaps have some trusted male friends who are married to her friends relate some of her most interesting traits. It sounds a bit awkward, but go ahead and ask them.

- Go on a personal hunt to find the best twenty to thirty most endearing qualities about her from another person's perspectives.

- If this seems to be a strange exercise, look at it this way: These questions are intended for these friends to share lovely qualities about a very special person. Perhaps they will even confide to other people what a great person she is. And who is the person generating all this great "publicity" about this special woman? Her loving husband! Again, keep your wife's best interest at heart.

OK, so the homework is underway. Let's get the fundamental plan development laid out. Now it is time to craft the extended sensuous buildup: *all day foreplay from "nine to five" and beyond*. Here is one blueprint to create the strategy for taking sexual enticement to the next level!

All Day Enticement: Build The Excitement

Delicious foreplay lingers and entices her all day through countless assorted skills. No matter which medium (texts, hand-written comments, emails, computer-generated notes, or provocative phone calls) is chosen, be sure to assure her loads of times that you love her. Expressing sincere, heartfelt affection through the word "love" communicates romance for her throughout the day. Think of the word "love" as a gentle thump upon her heart. These actions evoke strong emotions within her. The tease to please is always enjoyed when effectively delivered with genuine self-sacrifice with her pleasure in mind from the man she loves.

Reach out and touch her with specific

There are numerous methods to evoke this gradual excitement, as one example, strategic, calculated texts can build anticipation and intrigue. Create numerous texts distinctively calculated with her in mind to send tactically throughout the day. Some folks really enjoy the "racy" texts or "sexting," but for this beginning session, work to be as low key as possible. Think "*slow burn*" through this process from the time you leave for work until arrival back home. Begin with extremely moderate thoughts that gently stroke her emotions. Are there kids at home that she cares for during the day? She will most likely not want to see some X-rated text in the midst of feeding the kids or cleaning a mess that little "Johnny" has created for the tenth time today. This is a time to really serve her in extreme "Crock-Pot mode." These hints should occur in an unhurried manner so she will wonder when the heat is going to be dialed up a bit? The truth is, in this format, the heat will not to be turned up until you are just about to walk in the door and determine how her day actually progressed.

To provide a visual concept, look at the chart below to envision how to plot the texts in this gentle glowing fashion. The number "0" represents being cold, and "100" represents her being sexually steaming hot. The vertical line is the time of the day measured in whatever increments feel comfortable.

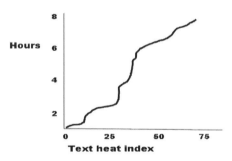

To recognize the mindset, this playfulness will not reach 100 until the end of the day after her slow-paced journey has been encouraged through the day, capped off with a bath, massage, or other physical activity to get her completely de-stressed from her daily activities. Remember that her needs are top priority, so this daylong foreplay contains deliberate plans enjoyed together only after the other preparations are finished culminating together in bed. If this is done according to these directions, she will not even get past the 50 heat range mark throughout the day from the texts until about two hours before returning home. Just like a Crock-Pot simmers all day on low heat, so the individual texts will create a slow, gradual increase to help her towards the eventual evening activities, which her mind and body need for true sexual fulfillment. This chart shows a picture of how the day might look with each new text on her mind.

Women enjoy being pursued by their lover.

The initial texts should speak of love focused upon her and about your being the most fortunate man on earth having her for a wife. If sending the texts in an orderly fashion, list out the messages to send to her beforehand, since adequate planning is fine. Focus attention on touching the inner walls of her heart with messages she can relate to. It is her heart that is the object for the pursuit. Women enjoy being pursued by their lover. A caution in this regard is to keep her heart, and not her genital region, as the target for the pursuit.

Before leaving home in the morning, create a bit of mystery and intrigue by leaving her a love note that says that today she will receive more texts than usual about her endearing qualities. Purposely make this note vague, but with a hint of today's fun. Learn to create an air of mystery since women enjoy intrigue. Her husband is the person who should instigate thrills into her day. Leave the note where she is sure to find it early on before getting onto her days activities.

In the initial texts, start with something like: "Have a great day! It will be great to wrap you in my arms tonight." Personalize these suggestions with expressions of warm feelings. Send her the information from one heart to another and not simply from one phone to another. Be specifically targeted in all the compliments aimed at her individuality. Do not say simply, "You look nice today." Rather, say something like, "You really look nice in that blue blouse; it makes your eyes look marvelous!" To promote a bit more intrigue, do not rush into sending the first text near the beginning of her morning. Build the anticipation mentioned in the note that was left for her. Wait a bit and increase the drama. PS – but don't forget to start sending the texts to her!

Start slow and build it up all day

Adapt these suggestions for the morning texts tempered to her life situation. Compile a list to be sent throughout the day working around some sort of structure like this:

> At first, tell her how much her work is appreciated, at home with the kids or at her job. Within the home, is she a good cook? Then make specific comments about her ability to make (whatever foods you genuinely enjoy)? Does she keep a nice house especially in spite of chasing kids every day? When it comes to "housework" or cooking, or something actually relating to the house or yard, what is it that she does better than any other wife? What are some detailed ways she serves the family? Create positive feelings within her by expressing unique qualities concerning her work at home. Keep these initial texts focused on her work concerning the home environment. Genuine compliments about a person's recognized work are always appreciated. It is OK to lavish them on a bit. As long as they are sincere compliments, toss on the topping! While it is OK to say, "Thank you for keeping the house so clean," it might be better to add, "It smells so nice to come home to such a clean house." Make them tailored to

her emotional mindset and the work she accomplishes to keep the house a home.

➢ Next, consider ideas about her "project management skills." Is she good at time management or does she "juggle" everything to get so much completed? Then let her know that managing her schedule is honestly appreciated. Some wives/mothers deal with their responsibilities better than anyone else in their church? Perhaps she takes care of the kids and does 100 added chores each week? Is she a true multitasker? Many women effectively control several projects simultaneously. Does she manage stress better than other people? Whatever her unique talents, tell her what makes her special!

➢ Find something exceptional about her in general, even mundane, daily activities to compliment her each day and especially on this special day of ***all-day foreplay***. Let her know that every feature of the marriage is appreciated. During the use of focused foreplay by text, mention a few of these special traits she possesses. Be imaginative and ask, "What was it about my wife that drew me to her in the first place?" Some husbands know right away what the unique answer will be concerning their wife. Some men have to think about it a bit. Either way, she has some very specific personal traits that make her extra special above all the women in the world. Jot down a list of these traits, and see how big the list can become. Keep the extra thoughts tucked away to express genuine appreciation for your special woman.

➢ What makes your wife laugh? Seriously, what touches her funny bone? Does she laugh at anything? Everything? When was the last time she just erupted in laughter? Why did she burst out like that? Use this information to reach in and touch her soul on this special day. Find some joke or a cartoon to share with her that will penetrate deep inside her heart. Find some cute picture of a life situation that will bring a smile to her face. Evoke shared memories perhaps brought on by something that happened on the way to work this morning. Did someone at the job say something that brought back a humorous event in your marriage?

These texts are to capture her essence and to tell her she is special

So, the initial text list is created, right? So now fashion the perfect scenario to text these compliments to her. Save this list, and make sure to mark which compliments are being sent today and which ones will be held for another time. There might be so many they might simply be randomly picked one at a time and sent to her "for no reason" except to make her day a bit better. Keep the romance and foreplay flowing even during days to just keep in touch and when not trying to become overtly sexual.

Begin to send out the texts at random time increments. Alternate between ones about her appearance, the home environment, or something humorous. This seems a bit contrived; however, if they can become very personally targeted, they will hit the mark. Stay personal, playful, and centered on her welfare.

Around noon, turn up the heat ever so slightly

This next set of texts is designed to get her thinking about her body image in a positive fashion. What are some of her best physical assets? Be sure she believes these are honest expressions about her or even a set of contrived steps to get in her pants. If she continually comments in a negative way about a certain part of her body, don't brush it off and think it won't matter to her. She is becoming more transparent regarding her sensitivity about something of specific interest or pain. Listen to the subtle messages she is sending. Create specific texts that target her sincere pain with your love.

These texts must be crafted with genuine admiration aimed at her heart.

"I wish you could see you through my eyes"

"Hey gorgeous, hope your day is fantastic! You are beautiful."

"I am looking forward to (pick one: sharing a cup of coffee with you, spending some time in the   kitchen helping with supper, watching you as I play with the kids, etc.) as soon as I get home as you are so easy on the eyes."

"I like the way (your blouse, your pants, your hair, etc.) looked this morning. That shade of (color of the article of clothing) looks nice on you." (If it happens to be a favorite blouse or shirt, tell her so.)

"Did you catch me peeping at your (body part) before I left the house? You are hot!"

"I enjoy inhaling your perfume. It makes my day start out so nicely on my mind"

Is your wife sexy? Tell her. Let her know she is sexy. She may deny it out loud, but her subconscious is being told that she is still desired by her husband. Many wives need tons of continual affirmations that she is worthy of being pursued. If a certain outfit is alluring, tell her. Think about her wardrobe, and let her know if a particular color or fashion is very enticing. Some wives are cautious about feeling "trashy" but at the same time want to be desired and maybe even a bit "naughty." Did she put on a show recently for her favorite one-person audience? Let her know how much it was appreciated. Discrete flashing for a private audience is mischievous but fun.

Has she recently been a bit playful with some brief glimpses of skin or even a blatant show on her part that was particularly pleasing? Compliment her desire to please. Fashion some texts that highlight those interesting times. These are still not "sexting," which some folks enjoy. The purpose for this set of texts is to emphasize her body as a pleasing image for her husband. Let her know that she is highly desired and prized!

About one hour before leaving work, turn up the heat a bit more

Gently nudge the temperature up a bit more for the afternoon. She should be getting the message by now as to where these messages are headed. This structured foreplay is to treat your wife as a queen and lover decidedly sought after by her husband. These are a bit more blatant but still not explicit. Perhaps re-craft these a bit to fit her personality:

"Can I schedule you as a spot on my to-do list tonight?"

"My hands miss your body, so many nice curves to explore"

"I noticed the (body part) that was flashed this morning. NICE!"

"You still get to me like the time we spent at (list some specific time or event that you   both enjoyed)." (If she has mentioned a certain trip, picnic or romantic outing, mention it   here to tie that experience into this evening.)

So, when you arrive home, now the questions to ask are: How is she doing? What type of a day has it been for her? How stressed is she or is she wondering what got into her husband today? Does she need to "unload" a bit concerning some incident or does she need to reconnect? If she shows a lot of interest in the various texts, act a bit coy, and just indicate that she was at the forefront your thoughts. Always be truthful while expressing that her needs are primary.

Look around to see what is needed to get dinner on the table or get the table set in the first place. Perhaps something needs attention, such as laundry, dishes, trash, etc. Involve the children, as this is great training about shared family responsibilities. Whatever she needs to make her load a bit lighter, do it. If the normal routine is to come in, give her a quick kiss, and go to the man cave, alter the routine somewhat. Start a new habit to look for ways to serve first, and then seek unwind time. Make special efforts to share the workload every day.

Because even the best laid plans can go awry, be prepared to spend time serving her needs upon first arriving home. If the children rush to get hugs and receive affection when the door is opened, as gently as possible, let them know that the first hug and kiss is reserved for the queen of the house. Be genuine, but gush it up a bit and let everyone know that she is first priority. Her actions may even deflect these gestures, but push through the maze, and greet her as though no one else is there. She is of primary importance upon getting back home.

Send a stronger sexual message by some physical touching. On every occasion possible, if she is not too stressed out, "accidently" on purpose bump into her or brush against her. Touch her arm or flip her hair a bit breathing in her fragrances coupled with a soft moan or express the pleasure derived from inhaling her fragrance. Give her a quick kiss on the neck or take her hand and gently place a very light kiss in between some of the work she is doing. If there are kids, express to them some form of compliment about their mom. It is also telling when the compliment is directed at "your wife" and not simply their "mom." Be open about affection to show children the proper way a husband and wife share their affection for each other. If they are teenagers, they should blush a bit by the overt show of affection.

Even though the rise in heat is gradual, this sets the stage for her to think about the frisky events to take place later on while dealing with the immediate pressures facing her. What does she need to be completely at ease emotionally tonight? Is there something else she needs to handle before she can shut down for the night? Determine if some item is blocking her complete relaxation. She may not be getting past something affecting her thoughts for later tonight. Help her become clear minded and focused.

After supper and before getting too tired in the evening

Now is the time to do whatever she needs to become completely relaxed and ready for your nighttime sexual activity.

❖ Does she need to read or work on the computer for a while to leisurely see what is happening with friends or family? Does she have a hobby that gets pushed to the back burner because of all the other items on the "to-do list"? What is it she needs to transition between the day and tonight?

❖ Would she enjoy a scalp massage or a foot rub to unwind? How often is her head massaged? If she gets headaches or has sinus trouble, a thoughtful, kind head massage might help. Work on the sides of her head, being cautious around the temples, as they are soft and sensitive. Most people omit the ears as a subject for the head massage. However, working behind and under each ear can provide extreme comfort. Pressing in on the center of her ear itself can increase the good feeling. Have fun and experiment.

❖ If she is ticklish on her feet, a stronger massage is pleasing. Rotate her feet and rub in between her toes. The tactile sensations from either a foot rub or a head massage is very pleasurable. Additionally, some women enjoy getting their hands massaged, emphasizing each finger and joint.

❖ Does she enjoy or need a bath to unwind? If so, how about specific reading or some favorite mood music? Would she appreciate a certain fragrance in the air or some particular candles? Keep in mind that a bath for men often gets us so relaxed we only want to sleep. She is not a man and may enjoy the bath to soothe away the day's stress. She needs to be as much at rest and peaceful as possible to appreciate sexual activity. Women typically desire the world being so far away from their mind that they have tranquility on the forefront of their thoughts.

❖ Is a back or full-body massage what she needs? This can serve multiple purposes. She might enjoy having the tensions from the day eliminated from her muscles through a sensual massage. As the massage is administered, this is a time for intimate, free-flowing conversation about the day or purely the physical connection of hands on her skin. Special fragrant massage oil is a nice addition, especially if your hands are rough. Subtle suggestions about the next step for the evening are enjoyable as you maneuver across her body. Naturally, muscular hands all over her skin bonds husband and wife physically, but for her, it also bonds at the emotional level as well. Take note of body language from her muscles or from the moans and ahhs she emits when a specific tension is eliminated or a certain muscle is massaged. Most times, a positive response by her means to remain right there and continue what is being done to her rather than moving on to some other place. Linger a while until that spot is properly rubbed down. How this ends should depend on her response. Ask open-ended questions with her needs in mind.

The sexual act itself will be covered in chapter nine. Though different from times of separation, some days might have extended foreplay while the day is spent together. Here are a few short examples for consideration regarding other ways to enjoy each other during a day with each other.

Physical Foreplay: Touching Her Body All During The Day Together

A different day of **extended foreplay** when together for the entire day:

Tantalizing enticement is not about obvious groping or touching her obvious erogenous parts: breasts and genitals. As was shown earlier, these activities are meant for slow, subtle, lingering, almost accidental caresses across many spots that are non-erogenous, as thought of by men. When women read this last statement, they wrinkle their brow a bit, as it seems to be another foreign concept to them – "non-erogenous spots." Their skin is the largest single exposed erogenous zone. To put it bluntly for the male perspective, it is as though each nerve were directly connected to the clitoris. It is not exactly that way, but for a man's understanding, her entire skin's surface is an erogenous area that excites a woman, but it needs artful stimulation for her to become effectively aroused.

Light strokes and subtle physical contact that convey that she is on his mind will usually become very arousing for a woman. The longer a couple is married, the more "indirect stimulation" a woman needs to reach a similar excitement as previous sexual encounters. Each husband and each wife is unique. This information covers the general ideas for a married couple.

This subtle physical stimulation entices her through the entire day. Husbands should flirt with their wife when they want to participate in foreplay and when they just want to send the message that they enjoy being with her. Flirting should not be omitted from a couple's activities simply because they are married. Actually, it should be practiced more since the restraints for each other's bodies are lifted. Here are a few ideas that need personal adaptation so that the relationship and personal experiences that the wife and husband can actively flirt with each other. His flirting should inspire her enticing responses back towards him.

First let's define "flirting" and then make some suggestions for creative flirting. Flirting is the **art of attracting your wife with subtle words and gestures**. Be on the alert for new ways to attract her. She desires intimate attention, so flirting is a perfect way to convey in her language that being with her is enjoyable. This process has many "heat ranges" from gentle accidental gestures all the way to blatant intimate groping. Most women seem to enjoy the subtle kind demonstrations normally associated with flirting more than the strong direct stimulation. In itself, flirting is a means to an end and not an end in itself. This intimate behavior conveys that being with her is an incredibly pleasant experience. Her increasing pleasure is the intent of flirting.

Flirting is the subtle way to express the joy-filled memories about first meeting one another. It can be his personal form of playful communication to indicate the developing attraction to her and her love. The emphasis is upon indirect and tantalizing and not on overt stroking.

Many women prefer to be caressed, touched, and gently kissed in a glancing fashion to stay connected with their husband, whether it is for romance or foreplay. So, if he were to subtly contact her two to three hundred times in a day while they were out together, without touching her breasts or genital area, she might become extremely turned on sexually. If he effectively stimulates her mind at the same time, she might appear a bit sex crazed. As mentioned earlier, women are aroused from the inside out when softly physically touched. The entire female skin area is a receptor comprised of millions of contact nerve points. Properly aroused, her skin wakes up her complete body, mind included. Even if this sounds a bit clinical, men should reflect on her need for "inside-out" stimulation over an extended time frame to become properly excited. Alternate these suggestions, and do not make them mechanical in nature. Thrill in the touch of her skin.

Physical caressing on every part of her body is a pleasant experience for women. So engaging in playful squeezes, long hugs, and affectionate soft kisses, indicates to her, "I am glad to be with you!"

Here are a few ideas to mix and match:

❖ Touch her thigh lightly, especially if she is wearing a skirt. However it is enticing for her even through her cloth. Run your fingers across her arm. Have you ever noticed just how sensitive she is on the inside bend of her arm? Inside her forearm? Listen to her as you touch any part of her body. Make a game of it, especially when all day is to be invested with each other.

❖ Kiss the back of her hand numerous times simply because her hand is very inviting and she is your bride. When she asks why you do it so often, tell her it is because you cannot keep your lips off her body. Let the innuendo linger with her. Kiss her ears and her chin just to stay close to her and if she has on perfume that is very pleasant Tell her she smells so good. These kisses should not be to run a trail down her neck to her cleavage. Enjoy every inch of her neck with light kisses every now and then just to enjoy her skin.

❖ Turn her head gently and give her seven or eight pecks around the outside of her mouth. When you stop, pause at first and look her in the eyes and tell her you cannot get enough of her.

❖ Tell her at least sixteen times during this special day "I love you," and if necessary, keep count. It will be worth it.

❖ Later in the day, after many, many touches in the discrete body parts listed above, turn up the heat by becoming a bit more daring as privacy allows. Touching her intimately when alone with her in the car or perhaps around the corner before appearing back with the crowd can be especially arousing. Understand the comfort level for her, as some wives are distracted by public displays of affection displays rather than becoming aroused. This is not a time to throw a "wet blanket" on the day's fun because you want to insist on some form of public display of affection where she is embarrassed. However, if she is up for various forms of discrete, naughty enticement, this can become a very exciting afternoon! Private intimacy will fire up the emotional and sexual flames.

Here were just presented two different forms for ***All-Day Foreplay*** for a husband and his wife. Mix and match these thoughts to blend a thoughtful dedication for your wife. On our website are listed many other methods to incorporate continuous foreplay to be incorporated into a marriage. No matter how long a couple has been married, foreplay never goes out of style. Seek every way possible to keep the marriage relationship fresh, vibrant, and brimming with new, wonderful ways to keep the spark alive!

You will see these two PEP PILLS to keep foreplay an all-day or even a weeklong event.

PEP PILLS for *All Day Foreplay* In Your Marriage: Action Steps For A Better Marriage Relationship

 # 1 – Another way to "reach out and touch her" without being with her all day: Place little notes for her to find that ask her to text you at a certain time of the day for clues for the nighttime activity. She has to send some form of the note back so you know she has found the particular note. Perhaps you make some "secret code" like a computer passwords that contain a gobbledygook of letters, numbers, and signs. Make it a special game between you two. Only send her the next text clue at a given interval after receiving her message and code. Set the interval time according to how many clues were hidden. Don't make the hiding places too easy or extremely hard to find. If they are too easy, she might find the notes before she should locate them in a particular sequence. The first notes need to be as moderate as the initial texts generated earlier in this chapter.

 # 2 – Find a way to lovingly touch your wife seven times during the day non-sexually every day for a month. As mentioned earlier, this is not touching her on her breasts or genital area, but rather on her neck, shoulder, arm, hair or feet. Just the mere practice of connecting with her in this manner will go a long way toward letting her know you value her and not just her body, even though you are touching her body. This may seem confusing, but try it and listen to how she mentions that you are more sensitive to her and it is emotionally reassuring for her. It may still seem foreign to appeal to her "non-erogenous" parts, which will in turn stimulate her sexually. As the saying goes, "Try it; you'll like it!"

Many women need lots of "non-sexual" touching to produce a desire for sexual activity. The emphasis here is to get your wife ready for sexual touching and more by way of her mind. Non-sexual touching to a woman is an emotional connection without being overtly sexual in nature. It is as if you are hinting in a subtle fashion that you want to "have her body" without saying those words directly to her.

Women need to emotionally bond with their husband several times throughout their day to be ready for his sexual advances later on. A wife wants quality time to get herself ready to receive her lover and to be with her intimately, mentally and physically.

Incorporate different days and more physically pleasurable ideas for her to include: an offer to massage her feet or shoulders or a pleasurable bath all by herself (add any specific oils or soap she likes and set the mood with her favorite music).

The next chapter discusses mutual sexual fulfillment. If time was spent focusing on her needs during a day or week of foreplay through the slow-burn method of all-day foreplay, she will really enjoy the culmination of the intimate physical time that awaits her that evening.

Always expect the best for your marriage!

CHAPTER 9

Sexual Fulfillment For Both Partners

No respectful marriage book aimed towards men would omit a chapter about SEX! There remains a definite separation between male and female expectations concerning sexual relations. The root problem in this area of marriage is that many women want lots of "non-sexual" touching to get ready for sexual activity and men do not understand or appreciate this dynamic about her physical and emotional make up. There will be many communication moments found throughout this chapter. Be sure to highlight them for interactive discussions.

Please, notice that this chapter is titled "*Sexual Fulfillment*" and not sex *techniques*. There are books galore that instruct couples how to try new positions and techniques together, ranging from the tame to the hot and embarrassing. There will be a few concepts for a husband to learn about his wife's body from this chapter. **Cracking The Marriage Code: PEP UP YOUR MARRIAGE** is designed to create the most glorious marriage possible for a husband and his bride from weekly dating, to the wonderful intimate experiences on their marriage bed (or other private location!). Guiding a couple for fulfilling the sexual dreams between a husband and his wife is the purpose here. As in every other chapter of this book, communication is the initial action step for a satisfying sexual relationship. Find out her stages for sexual excitement and fulfillment. Does she require several days to become sexually excited? How much non-sexual touching and intimate communication does she require for the maximum benefit for her?

> If your wife is not relaxed,
> she will not enjoy high-
> quality sex.

So, a man might ask, "How can non-sexual touching get a woman ready for sexual touching and pleasure?" Was this the *FIRST* chapter on the must read list? If so, be sure to check out at least chapters seven, **"Nourishing Romance,"** and eight, **"Nine-to-Five Foreplay,"** so there is a basis for the information presented to understand a bit more about a woman's inner workings. Just as this book has listening skills and foreplay before sexual fulfillment, a wife wants these principals in that same order! A husband needs to speak with his wife about these dynamic emotional centers.

Ironically, in the area of sexual enjoyment, my parents had a better grasp on the reasons for sexual intimacy than did Elaine's parents, at least in what they related in "the talk" to the two of us respectively. My parents mentioned that sexual enjoyment is for both partners' pleasure, and Elaine's teaching was that sex was a duty for the wife to perform for her husband. At least that was her impression from her upbringing. My parents did not understand the complete commitment between a husband and his wife, so one effective segment does not make a whole marriage successful. As a married couple, due to this misunderstanding, Elaine and I struggled as a couple for many of our first years of marriage. It is refreshing to see many Christian blogs openly talking about a satisfying sexual relationship being a gift from God. God created sex to be enjoyed freely between a man and a woman in the covenant of marriage, even as He created us male and female.

Unfortunately, many Christians or churches have taught so firmly against sex before marriage, that young people grow up believing that any sex is wrong. It is not sex that is wrong. It should be taught that, **in the proper environment of marriage, sex is glorious and fun**!

It's OK. People Know That Married Couples Have Sex!

It may be surprising to our younger readers that their parents and some couples in between these two generations were not so open concerning sexual activities for married couples, especially among "Christians." One woman at our seminars did not want her husband to go to the front of their church to ask for prayer so they might have a child. When asked why she was so nervous about her request, her reply was: "Then they will know we are having sex!"

To the younger couples, congratulations, the door of communication about things sexual has been opened. Perhaps it is due to the many social issues that make the front page or the various electronic media experiences today. Whatever the reasons, it is a good sign that younger married couples will talk about sex more openly than did their parents' generation. And do not bring up what their grandparents would not discuss!

This is not to say that sex has always been a "never discussed" issue. Growing up in the sixties in Florida, it was an often-talked-about subject. There are many fine marriage blogs and wholesome books that show the godly side of sexual practices. Still, many folks have questions concerning sex and the various issues suffered by couples today. Too many couples do not understand the problems that surface from not speaking frankly with their spouse concerning sexual issues.

What *Sexual* Baggage Should Become a Topic for a Wife and her Husband to Discuss?

Kindness and sensitivity go a long way in this emotionally charged discussion. The issues of "baggage" indicate an emotional scar or wound in either spouse. Let her know that you are willing to share her burden if that is what she needs. Be sure you understand Chapter Five on "Listening Skills" here to be tuned into her needs and not your pride.

Baggage creates a useful emotional picture as people come to a relationship with all sorts of sizes, shapes, and colors of problems. These discussions can lead to enhancing your relationship quicker than you can imagine.

For emphasis, let me repeat, **BE SENSITIVE** to her emotions. Have tissues close by, and give her time to share her heart. You are looking to help her heal in this area of her life. That does not mean you need to generate five or six solutions to her problems. Healing may be developed from her exposing a sensitive area from her past. Listen and allow her to give you any details she wants whenever she wants and at her pace. Be sure you have her issues at the center of this discussion. She may only need to give you details without your commentary or judgment. Think of her at this point as a gentle flower just beginning to open its petals to the world. She is fragile and needs extreme sensitivity, not a correcting spouse. Be in the moment for her and allow her to tell you anything she wants to.

This might give you a time to share some of your sexual issues. Do not come across as bragging or comparing your past with whom you have now. Let your wife know that you want to be honest and yet not injure her. You need her help in handling an issue you have been weighed down with.

A Satisfying Sex Life is Developed as a Husband and a Wife Surrender Themselves to One Another

Satisfying sex is *not* about recreating some exotic oriental technique or specific position on numerous occasions that brings her some "over the top climax." Fully satisfying sex is not achieved because a certain technique or pattern of body movements was executed a certain way during the last interlude and therefore it must be repeated. **Satisfying sexual enjoyment is about the pleasure of the husband and his wife experiencing a physical and spiritual relationship they were designed to enjoy.** Yes, both sexes were "DESIGNED" to enjoy a satisfying physical relationship.

This is not to belittling any new methods and skills a couple can learn from various books and blogs. I strongly encourage every married couple to get more information about sexual gratification for their mutual pleasure. However, do not reduce married sexual passion to the right skill set of "insert tab A into slot B." For most women, it is all in how emotionally and intimately prepared she is before they enter into the actual sexual activity itself.

A couple's sexual gratification is about the entire journey to fulfillment and only not about the last-minute method for a particular nightly engagement. Quickie sex will be covered a bit later so the emphasis within this information is mutual sexual satisfaction. A wise husband will focus on bringing his wife along the journey from initial communications about his intentions to the mutual release for each partner according to her timing. Her satisfaction should be his ultimate goal. Many wives enjoy intercourse AFTER they have reached their initial orgasm. Each partner enjoys different aspects of the sexual journey.

> It may surprise many wives that their husband's greatest pleasure is found through *HER SATISFACTION* and not simply due to his climax.

He wants to see his wife basking in the glow of a fulfilled sexual euphoria every time they enjoy their physical intimacy. While this is not possible every time, he should set this as his goal. A caring husband learns to incorporate enough foreplay to prepare his wife for her pleasure. A substantial point for husbands is that **her orgasm or climax is not always her end goal**. As strange as that sounds to men, many wives enjoy the journey towards the sexual union as more important than the few seconds of euphoric release. Since some women are not able to reach orgasm for one reason or another, the intimate journey and the couple's shared pleasurable intimacy is very often her goal. Yet for the man, climax is the ultimate goal to a wonderful sexual fulfillment experience. Does this opposing set of intimate goals create some problems in so many bedrooms because of these unmatched expectations? A wise husband will seek his wife's feelings about her body relative to their sexual interactions.

Sex Should Always be Something You're Doing with Her, not to Her

How a caring husband helps his wife become aroused and passionate will go farther towards generating a fulfilling sexual experience for her than he might understand. Don't be selfish; give her what she needs to be sexually excited and fulfilled. A man and a woman have different agendas when it comes to a fulfilling sexual experience. So knowing what turns her on is critical to their mutual sexual experience. Be sure to talk about the shared expectations and possible agendas. We fellows tend to think on a simple path towards the end goal where your wife is looking for the journey to be romantically lined with soft words and gentle touches that nudge her towards the bed. Focus on her needs as the primary thoughts in your process.

Keep in mind the adage "ladies first" when you are working towards your ultimate result. Does she need a varied approach for each encounter due to her daily activities and stresses? To be good in bed it's not enough to memorize "routines" to be repeated like two robots performing mechanical duties. He needs the right mindset long before they enter the bedroom. No matter the style of sexual preference, sex should always be something you're doing with her, not to her. Too many times men feel as though they are doing an act to their wife. Have you heard your wife comment that for her *it was a sexual experience* and not just some mechanical exchange of fluids? That sentence even sounds foreign, doesn't it? Listen to women speaking about the atmosphere that surrounds the sexual act itself. They will express "emotional connection," "romantic interludes," or some form of relationship experience. It is truly a bonding relationship for women and begins long before the bedroom act happens.

Sexual Pleasure is not a Race; It is a Delightful Destination

Her pleasure should be a husband's ultimate target. As mentioned in Chapter Eight, extended foreplay should be the normal procedure to get your wife's mind to the experience long before joining physically. A wise husband will continue to learn how to stimulate his wife's body for her ultimate stimulation. Take it slow rather than charging quickly towards the end result of personal release. If it has been a few days since your last sexual interlude, keep extremely focused on her satisfaction, since your body is screaming "speed." Be sure to express to her that her pleasure is the goal, not some new technique, unless some new technique has been recently mutually discussed. She needs to know without any hesitation that her timing and her body is the gauge being used to determine the night's sexual timeframe. When a husband does not tune into his wife's needs, she can feel used as an object for his sexual release rather than being the focus for a pleasurable encounter. When her emotional and physical needs are met, in that order, she feels validated as his bride. Which way should a caring husband treat his wife? Keep in mind that this is a time for mutual sexual pleasure; it is not a race.

Observe her body movements. Listen to her interest level. Feel her mood as well as her words. Does she need more slow touching or back scratching? What is going on within her is more a signal for you to proceed than are her smile or her normal methods of stimulation. Is her body responding to a specific touch? Is she moaning or purring a bit? Listen to "HOW" she responds to your touch. When you are doing something right, her body will move or she might tremble to say you are doing a good job.

From all the articles, women's public feedback, and our interaction with couples, we know that most men take their wife's pleasant expressions as a signal to move onto another motion or touch. This is not what she is saying to you. Stay and continue the lovely activity that she is enjoying.

IMPORTANT NOTE TO MEN: When your wife tells you that something you are doing feels good, this is a signal to keep doing what you are doing. It is not a signal to move on to another stroke or move to a different place on her body. This is a significant rule all the way through your lovemaking. For instance, when you are massaging her breasts or when you finally start touching her clitoris and she says, "That feels really good," do not stop what you are doing.

Notice when she guides your hands or moves her body into a different position. These are signs for you to follow her lead. If she lies fairly motionless, you need to be subtle but aware of her desires. What is her body telling you? What does she need to get to the next plateau?

ANOTHER IMPORTANT NOTE TO MEN: She wants you to take the lead. However, she will give slight indications to guide you, and you should follow her movements. Watch her body, is she beginning to tremble or squirm or writhe?

You can quietly and softly ask for loving directions. If she does not enjoy speaking during this heated foreplay, listen to her body, and do not push the issue for her to speak verbally. Some women become distracted when they want to enjoy the journey. Start rubbing or massaging where you know she enjoys the pleasure she is receiving. All through the sex "dance," be sure to tune into her body response, and listen to her words, moans, and breathing as a means to get feedback from her. Enjoy the reactions as you watch her body respond to gentle touches and kisses.

Sexual Fulfillment is a Passionate Familiarity That Two People Physically Share at Their Most Intimate Level

Sometime it is about being spontaneous, and then for other times, it means keeping to a schedule. If there are children at home, women do not want to think that the kids know mom and dad are physically intimate. Therefore, it may be for the best to plan or schedule sex due to all the other activities for the family. No matter what is decided upon, couples need to give each other the space to enjoy their individual experiences together within the framework of their comfort levels, all the while squeezing in your times to be physical with each other. As in every other area of a marriage, true open communication is the pathway to each partner having a fulfilling sex life.

Husbands, spend an extended time kissing her

This is not to rule out oral sex; it is simply to include a practice many husbands seem to lose interest in, according to many wives. It seems that husbands do not understand how much women enjoy the pleasure of kissing. Husbands need to learn how to tease her with the tongue and lips.

There are different styles and types of kisses. Soft almost glancing touches create sensitivity wherever her skin is contacted. A trail of light contacts can begin on one side and go in many directions landing on the opposite side of her body. Use your lips to stimulate her skin, and try to create as many "goose bumps" as possible along the way. Mix the type, pace, and firmness of strokes to keep her guessing what is next.

Alternate between different body parts, and go back to her lips and start all over in another direction. Continue to listen to her inner groaning or pleasant sounds, and feel her body respond to each touch. Vary the intensity and the timing as your lips explore her body.

Vary the sexual activities and determine what she wants as to heated foreplay:

➢ How much does she enjoy having her breasts stimulated? Does she enjoy your hands a bit softer or somewhat firmer? How does she touch her own breasts? What she does to herself is the most pleasant, so imitate her movements.

➢ Combine lips, hands, and body movements to create more stimulation over her entire body.

➤ If she has a massager or vibrator, either one could be incorporated to change up the variety of accelerated pleasures. (If toys are uncomfortable for your marriage, it is Ok to not have them.)

➤ When you eventually reach her lower erogenous areas around her vagina, do not pounce directly onto her very sensitive clitoris. Women were created with thousands of highly sensitive nerve endings all across her skin. While the clitoris is the most sensitive concentrated area on her body, all of her body is interconnected and needs stimulation. Take the time to explore her body as the marvelous creation before you. The areas just above and just below her vagina are very attuned to your touch, whether by the fingers, lips, or other body parts. Make a wonderful process of seeing how much can be contacted on her skin around the "marvelous button" without direct stimulus. Enjoy the wonders of her body and listen to her responses.

➤ Does she need constant clitoral stimulation once you start? Her answer may surprise her husband. She will give signs that your intensity can be dialed up or down. Women often require *less direct pressure* on their clitoris as they become extremely aroused. This wonderful organ, designed exclusively for her pleasure, becomes more sensitive when aroused. Unlike a man's penis, which requires a more firm stimulation and a stronger grip as he gets closer to orgasm, she may enjoy a light, almost imperceptible touch as she progresses. This is another wonderful opposite distinction between most men and women. A wise husband is sensitive to his wife's body language as she draws to her first orgasm. The massive enjoyment for a shrewd husband is in the learning process of his wife's wondrous bodily evolution.

➤ Is oral stimulation something she enjoys as foreplay, or does she need to climax first from oral sex to enjoy her greatest pleasure through intercourse? **NOTE:** For men this may seem strange; however, many women confess that they are not as ready to participate in intercourse until they have one or more oral or hand-stimulated orgasms. Remember, her pleasure first. How can she become the most aroused tonight? Each interlude will be unique, and she may change her desires as the night progresses. Be attentive to how her body is responding.

➤ Some nights she may be ready for intercourse much faster, but keep in mind that she sets the pace.

➤ Oral sex to climax alone may be her need for this particular time. Why do the female parts enjoy the tongue more than the fingers? Perhaps it is due to the relative softness?

These are just a few brief scenarios for consideration. Be ultra sensitive to what she needs. Your wife may not give specific indications before the passion builds between you two during each occurrence. Learn to "read her body language" on the fly and enjoy the continuous changes that each lovemaking session provides. Each episode can awaken a new experience. Unfortunately, all couples drift into the comfortable, and a certain routine will eventually become the default occurrence.

Quickies are those wondrous special times when either or both partners **NEED SΣX NOW!** It takes many forms, sometimes incorporating hidden remote places for extra excitement.

* Are the kids taking a nap? Slip off together!

* Perhaps someone is coming to dinner or a visit in a short time and one of you thinks it would be fun to fit in a quick interlude before the guests arrive. It will add some spice to the discussion as the events from a short time ago lingers in your minds.

* Sometimes one partner needs sexual release, and the other spouse is too tired or too distracted to engage in normal, lengthy foreplay and sexual activity. Why not provide them with a quick answer to their problem?

Remaining sensitive to each other's desires and acting on that intimate insight for the other spouse's best interest is how a marriage grows. Speedy sex is one way to keep the excitement active. The usual disclaimers abound. Do not do anything illegal. Recreating some teenage fantasy may add fun, but it may also be against the law. However, you could enjoy sex in the garage or on the patio since you have a fenced-in yard. No need to go back into the bedroom, enjoy each other in some other room of the house. Use your imagination and enjoy each other spontaneously. These special times should not become the norm, but they add an interesting zest to a couple's activities.

With that being said, "quickies" can add an electric-type shock to a husband and his wife's stagnant sex life. There are many ways to engage in these endeavors that are legal and rekindle a youthful enthusiasm for both partners. Any way in which husbands and wives can add zest to their marriage with different sexual practices is encouraged.

The Lifetime Target for a Husband Should be to Enrich his Wife's Sexual Experience

When either partner is not satisfied with the "default settings" for sexual fulfillment, one person has to initiate the changes. Be considerate of events going on in both your worlds, yet be open to try new sexual experiences that never cross the lines for each spouse's moral standing. Each spouse has separate reasons for the regular sexual experiences they enjoy. While each encounter is dissimilar from all the others, they need to take pleasure in variety by changing their sexual practices with various times of the day, or varieties of actions and multiple positions to be enjoyed apart from the fluid life experiences that bombard every couple.

A husband's pleasurable job is to lovingly stimulate his wife for her pleasure. Keep in mind that the focus for this book is to help a husband understand and communicate with his wife in every aspect of marriage. This is never more important for him than in their mutual sexual pleasures. How tame or how wild your personal experiences occur is dependent on how you help each other arrive at the pleasure you both seek. Wives can also initiate these sexual practices and teach their husbands to more fully understand her body. No matter the ages for each spouse, sexual fulfillment can be a continuous learning experience overflowing with passionate satisfaction.

Few things are as pleasurable as the intense shared intimacy between a wife and her husband culminating in joyous sexual fulfillment. Deepen this marvelous shared intimacy through open communication, and always remember to have fun with each other! A bit of humor in the marriage bed makes the ride go much smoother! (Pun intended)

HAVE FUN WITH THESE *"PEP PILLS"* FOR YOUR MARRIAGE

Note – All of these discussion topics are to be handled outside the intimacy of your actual sexual activity. Please, do not try to bring up some emotional or physical issue that may present a problem while you are in the midst of passion. Set time aside, and let her know there is something important to discuss with her privately. No matter what is discovered today, her body, including her emotional well-being, might change tomorrow.

She will not become disappointed with your prowess if some personal "move" is not as successful tonight as it was the last three times you had sex. Her body does not respond the same way each time to the same stimulus since that is not how she was made. Enjoy the constant changes, and benefit from the journey!

Approaching these discussions require preparation and sensitivity. **Think through these first questions prior to the "PEP PILLS" themselves.**

❖ What was your wife's background teaching regarding sex within a marriage? What was yours?

❖ Does she enjoy or endure sex? Sometimes wives want to please their husband so they have "duty sex." Do not assume she has shared her most inner secrets so far simply because she has let you into her physically. Some wives take a long time to fully let down their emotional guard. A husband should build up a wall of protection for her to share any and everything she feels comfortable telling her best friend.

❖ How often does she "fake an orgasm" to keep you from feeling inadequate? This is a common occurrence in many marriages. Don't let it cause a rift, but allow it to open the communication floodgates for your marriage. For a wife to fake an orgasm to "please her husband" is a lie and can damage their relationship. It is serious enough to carve out the time to give your wife the opportunity to honestly share her emotional and physical preferences.

Due to the delicate nature of sex between a husband and his wife, here are some extra exercises in this section.

Now on to the exercises. There are many ways that a couple can spice up their sex life, but they should always be discussed: The PEP PILLS for Sexual Fulfillment :

1 – What does a husband need to understand about his wife's expectations and sexual fulfillment?

What does your wife expect from sexual activities? Does she want to experience orgasm, or does she want to enjoy shared intimacy and enjoy **your climax**? As foreign as it seems to men, not all women experience an orgasm each time they have sex. A husband will eliminate many frustrating sessions between him and his wife if he talks about this dynamic early and often in their marriage. If you have been together a long time and have not actually approached this subject, do so as soon as it is convenient to discuss such a sensitive issue.

Do not feel that her not having a climax is "your fault." Some women do not achieve a climax every time, and they are perfectly happy that way. This does not mean they do not enjoy the mutual sexual experience; it means a woman is different than a man. Her pleasure should remain as the primary typical daily focus so you will both have a more enjoyable sexual time. To open the conversation a bit, here are a few questions to ask:

- What is the most erotic adventure we could experience together?

- What is the ideal number of times to have sex per week or per month?

- Do you have an orgasm every time we make love?

- Is it necessary for me to try to help you have an orgasm each time?

2 – With *HER* Sexual Fulfillment in mind, what does she need from you to be ready for you?

- How can you best serve her needs to help her experience all that God designed in   her?

- Ask your wife to be very specific and to tell you at least five or six examples of what non-sexual touching means to her. You might be greatly surprised at her answers.

- To stretch the discussion a bit, ask her:

- Is there a sexual fantasy you will share with me?

- Is there a sexual secret you haven't told me, yet feel comfortable now sharing?

- What are some of the most amazing aspects of our sex so far?

- How can I better serve your sexual needs?

3 – What do you know about each other's past family teaching?

- Discuss each set of parents' differences as it relates to sex?

- Spend some evenings asking some questions like these:

- What do you remember your parents telling you about sex?

- Do you recall any "taboos" they placed on married couples?

- Was there any sexual teaching or advice shared?

4 – What new experiences would be mutually enjoyable for your sexual occurrences?

Take time to speak with her about:

- New places, techniques, or positions for sex.

- Oral sex, masturbation, or any other type of sex act that is not part of the normal sexual experience.

- Does she need (want) oral pleasure in order to become ready for you to enter her, or is oral to orgasm her desire? Does she need an oral, hand-stimulated or toy-induced orgasm to be ready for intercourse?

- What fears is she keeping a secret?

- "What do you think we could do to make our sex life more exciting?"

- "Of all that I do to provide sexual satisfaction, what turns you on the most?"

Where there is tension about some subject for intimate discussion, these very subjects can become effective areas to cultivate the relationship. A couple may be embarrassed about these sensitive subjects, but it is better to be a bit embarrassed and discuss them, than to be comfortable in ignorance. Great marriages flourish from active, open communication about any subject, no matter how sensitive the topic.

When sensitive issues create tension, be responsive to each other's needs and wants, but make the effort to discuss these problems together. When problematic concerns do not violate any core beliefs, why have such hesitancy in speaking about them or bringing new skills to the lovemaking experience? Be careful and sensitive, as there could be deep-seated ideas lurking in her mind that needs gentle nurturing and thoughtful understanding to come to the surface.

When it comes to sexual performance, husbands and wives are very different emotionally and physically, so appreciate the unique way that God designed you both.

Men can lay almost any personal concern aside for the chance at having satisfying sex with their wives. Women usually enjoy pleasure only after their mind and internal emotional "baggage" is relieved through compassionate conversation with a trusted friend. Become her most trusted ally in whatever her past looks like to relieve her of any negative issues she has.

Whenever a subject is perceived as "taboo," tenderly yet openly ask why it is so. It is not wrong to have different opinions about sex or sexual practices. Use these differences to draw closer in your marriage relationship. Do not allow any subject to be completely off the table for discussion, even when it is not something either person wants to include as a personal practice. Not employing a specific act together is all right, but it does not mean discussing it is to be avoided. Open communication in your sex life will be liberating for numerous other areas of marriage. You might find that how open you are in discussing sexual issues is in direct correlation to intimacy in other parts of the relationship.

Always Expect The Best For Your Marriage!

CHAPTER 10

THE BEGINNING: Injecting life into each other (even while the kids are home) ninety days at a time.

This final chapter is actually the beginning. This is a short chapter with a strong call to action to make your marriage the very best it can become. In your marriage arrange all that is presented through **Cracking The Marriage Code** by applying the principals learned through this book. Work at marriage in small increments of ninety days at a time. This section is primarily a call to action for any part of the book passed over or where extra work is needed.

✓ **Were all the PEP PILLS action exercises at the end of each chapter practiced?**

Go back through them, and work on the ones that were skipped, and redo all that were most enjoyed. Each action step is calculated to draw a husband and wife closer together through fun practical steps.

✓ **Life can be endured or enjoyed.** Each couple has the daily choice as to how they will fill up their time.

Assess where this journey has progressed and what can be achieved in the near future. How has your relationship grown over the past few weeks as the information washed over your marriage? Did each lesson build upon the previous as it was designed? How has the cycle of communication developed within your marriage? Does she trust you more today than a few months ago? Continue to deepen the confidence that is growing between you.

Understanding the difference between two particular words can increase sensitivity between a husband and his wife:

The first word is Empathy. Empathy is the capacity to recognize emotions that are being experienced by another. It is the ability to understand the other person's side of the discussion. To be empathic is to see her ideas and thoughts without taking it personally within the discussion. Empathy means the person is removed from the baggage carried by the other person. Husbands are able to step back and evaluate both frames of reference.

The second word is Sympathy. Sympathy is the capacity to share the pain with the person who is wrestling with the problem. A woman might be struggling with some childhood distress that haunts her. Another person who is sympathetic will feel her pain.

Very often, men share empathy more naturally, and women feel sympathy. Men can be sympathetic and women can be empathetic, but the natural response is for men to be empathetic. These concepts are presented to shed light on how people process information in their own way and why one person may respond to a given situation in a completely opposing manner than their spouse. This seeming contradictory response is not wrong; it is just not the same.

Men and women react to the same event with contradictory responses. How they each deal with these male/female wonders will determine how well their relationship flourishes.

The most important thought here is what is needed in your marriage. More empathy or sympathy? Or both? What your marriage will become is based upon actions that are taken today and each "today" forever. This section is designed to create a desire to always improve the marriage relationship for the better, each day and therefore, each week.

Where is your marriage relationship now and Where can it go from here?

Reviewing the chapters will reveal a natural progression for every marriage. Ponder just how to mesh the life experiences with all the various facets of your relationship from those early dating days to that special day at the altar all the way into the varied forms of intimacy within your physical sexual pleasurable times. Hopefully, it has been apparent that it is important to improve all verbal communications in every step along the way, since communication is the greatest answer for a smoother relationship between husband and wife.

Honestly examine any needed additional growth. This growth is the fun side to any bond, as it is how to develop the companionship and cherished connection people seek through their marriage. Marriage maturity is a reflection of mutual interactions between a husband and his wife for each other's improvement. Seek her best interest in every endeavor pursued in the marriage connection.

❖ How is the marriage connection right now?

❖ What constructive changes are needed in the future three months?

❖ What additional assistance could make it the best marriage it can become?

❖ Are there negative habits that need to be eliminated to promote a closer intimacy?

These questions can be used to create a personal list of changes that should take place in your marriage. What beneficial changes would they personally accomplish for the marriage? Keep in mind that a person cannot "change" another person. You can only work on yourself. So, the challenge is not to change your wife but to make continual personal corrections.

It is helpful if both partners work together to provide mutual joyful experiences. However, it can be enough for one partner to pave the way to a beautiful life experience by choosing to become all he or she is designed to become. The focus must be upon learning and implementing those learned principals to form healthy habits that in turn reshape new relationship muscles.

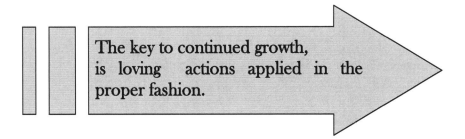

The key to continued growth, is loving actions applied in the proper fashion.

PEP PILLS For Creating The Best Marriage You Can Possibly Have: Action Steps For A Better Marriage Relationship

 # 1 – Ask your wife where she feels growth in you has occurred while reading and applying this book. When this question is asked, be ready for good dose of positive reinforcement. Ask what additional changes she feels would benefit the marriage.

Try to frame questions in the positive form rather than in the negative. For instance, it is not as good to ask, "Where do you feel I need to still make changes?" Instead, ask, "In what ways have I become a better husband over the past few weeks?" And "What changes could I make that would benefit the relationship?" The information is similar in substance; however, it is directing her to look for the best and not search for unconstructive matters.

Thank her for any constructive comments she makes, and listen carefully so any suggestions can be implemented soon. To gain extra mileage on this exercise, jot a handwritten note to her during the week following the discussion to let her know how much the insights were appreciated. It is a way to compliment her judgments.

 # 2 – Bring up any and all constructive changes in her behavior. Again, be sure to accentuate the positive characteristics. How has she changed recently in the marriage? Have you kept a running list of these personal gems? At an appropriate time, tell her how much her thoughts have meant. It is wonderful to see that she is also working on the marriage.

 # 3 – What special activities do you have planned? Be sure to carry through with those plans. Look back through the PEP PILLS and see the activities that are on the calendar for completion. What extra plans are needed? Perhaps there were a few romantic "getaways" tentatively scheduled where something prevented their accomplishment? Be sure they get back on the priority list and happen. Yes, life gets in the way at times, but make sure any special intimate plans are carried out. **The fringe benefits can be amazing!**

 # 4 – Please, take the time to let me know how I can better serve you and your wife?

Go to this website

www.JerryStumpf.com

Send us an email at

PepUpYourMarriage@hotmail.com

and share your story with us.

Follow us on Facebook :

https://www.facebook.com/crackingmarriagecode

- Tell us what improvements have been made to your marriage and how they have created a better relationship?

- What is needed from me to be covered for your relationship, either in any of these chapters or what needs to be addressed in another book or video series?

- If it would be helpful, a personal set of sessions can be arranged for the four of us (you two and my wife and myself) to meet in person online through a video conference call.

- How can I personally help you and your wife? This is my passion in life to divorce-proof marriages.

Be sure to email me since now you are part of a special inner circle of couples who have made the effort to create a lifetime of wonderful memories. **There are many free articles and even a few prizes for husbands to continue wooing their wife to be found on our various sites**

Always Expect The Best From Your Marriage!

18719453R00116

Made in the USA
Middletown, DE
18 March 2015